THE ARCHAEOLOGY
of
LANCASHIRE

PRESENT STATE *and* FUTURE PRIORITIES

edited by RICHARD NEWMAN

LANCASTER UNIVERSITY ARCHAEOLOGICAL UNIT

1996

ii

Published by
Lancaster University Archaeological Unit
Meeting House Lane
Storey Institute
Lancaster
LA1 1TH

Phone: (01524) 848666
Fax: (01524) 848606
Email: Archunit@Lancs.ac.uk
(*Internet:* World Wide Web URL: http://www.lancs.ac.uk/users/archaeol/unit/luau.htm)

Printed by
Kent Valley Colour Printers,
Kendal, Cumbria

ISBN 1-86220-010-6

Formatted and designed by R Middleton and R A Parkin
Illustrated by R Middleton and R Danks

Front cover: the Bleasdale circle, Forest of Bowland, Lancashire

CONTENTS

ACKNOWLEDGEMENTS

The editor wishes to thank all the contributors for taking part in the conference and for subsequently producing their texts and revisions to tight timetables. Bob Middleton is particularly thanked for undertaking much of the design work and producing the digitally-generated maps. Ruth Parkin undertook the final formatting of the camera-ready copy, and Dick Danks provided the additional manually-drawn illustrations.

The editor is also grateful to Peter Gunn for indexing the volume, and to John Dodds for assisting in its production. Especial thanks are owed to Peter Iles for making Sites and Monuments data available during the researching of the volume.

The conference and volume were part-funded by a grant from Lancashire County Council.

CONTRIBUTORS

David Shotter is a senior lecturer in the Department of History, Lancaster University, specialising in Roman History and numismatics. He is the author of numerous books on the Roman archaeology of the North West.

Ben Edwards was, until August 1995, the County Archaeological Officer for Lancashire. Ben is now Chairman of the Friends of the Lancaster University Archaeological Unit. He is author of a number of books and articles on archaeological subjects in Lancashire.

Ron Cowell is the Curator of Prehistoric Field Archaeology at the National Museums and Galleries on Merseyside. He is co-author of the *The Wetlands of Merseyside*, and has written extensively on early prehistory in the Merseyside area.

Robert Middleton is a Project Officer with the Lancaster University Archaeological Unit and has been one of the driving forces behind the North West Wetlands Survey project. He is co-author of the *The Wetlands of North Lancashire*.

Colin Haselgrove is a Professor of Archaeology at the University of Durham. His numerous publications on later prehistory include *Iron Age Coinage in South-East England: the Archaeological Context*.

Kath Buxton was a Project Officer with the Lancaster University Archaeological Unit until May 1996, when she joined English Heritage's Central Archaeology Service. Kath directed excavations at Ribchester and Kirkham.

Adrian Olivier was the Director of the Lancaster University Archaeological Unit until November 1993, when he became head of the Central Archaeology Service. Adrian directed excavations throughout the North West but notably at Walton-le-Dale and Ribchester. He is the author of English Heritage's *Frameworks for our Past*.

Rachel Newman is an Assistant Director with the Lancaster University Archaeological Unit. Rachel has directed sites throughout the North West, concentrating particularly on Post-Roman and Roman sites such as Dacre. She is Project Manager of the North West Wetlands Survey.

Richard Newman has been Director of the Lancaster University Archaeological Unit since May 1994. He is a former committee member of the Medieval Settlement Research Group and author of a number of articles on medieval settlement and heritage management.

Andrew White is Curator for Lancaster City Council Museum Services. An expert on medieval pottery and on urbanisation in the North West, he was editor of *A History of Lancaster 1193-1993.*

Jason Wood is an Assistant Director with the Lancaster University Archaeological Unit and a specialist in buildings archaeology. Jason has run projects on many major monuments in the North West including Lancaster Castle and Furness Abbey. He is editor of the Institute of Field Archaeologists' *Buildings Archaeology: Applications in Practice.*

Mark Fletcher has been a Project Manager with the Lancaster University Archaeological Unit since August 1994, before which he was a member of the Greater Manchester Archaeological Unit. Mark has directed many sites of all periods in historic Lancashire, but has a particular interest in industrial monuments.

Graeme Bell is Chief Planning Officer with Lancashire County Council and has been instrumental in securing an archaeological and curatorial service for Lancashire.

Peter Iles was, until April 1996, the Sites and Monuments Record Officer for the Lancaster University Heritage Planning Consultancy. With the transfer of the Sites and Monuments Record to Lancashire County Council he now fulfills the same role for them.

INTRODUCTION: THE STUDY OF LANCASHIRE'S PAST

by David Shotter

This publication results from a one-day conference on the Archaeology of Lancashire, organised by the Lancaster University Archaeological Unit (LUAU) and held in May 1995. Its purpose was to review the present state of our knowledge, and to pinpoint directions for future research. Each participant was asked to discuss a period or theme in the context of the geographical area embraced by the post-1974 county of Lancashire, or where such a division seemed too restrictive to focus on historic Lancashire. A major significance of the conference was that its audience was made up not just by those with a professional interest in the subject, but also consisted of representatives of local societies and schools, as well as committed individual hobby archaeologists — all people whose knowledge and interest make them an indispensable part of the 'research-team'. The discussion at the end of the day paid a considerable amount of attention to ways in which the diversity of interest might be brought together, spurred on by the observations of Graeme Bell, the County Planning Officer, summarised in the penultimate paper of this volume. Progress towards turning some of these observations into realities has been made in the interval between the conference and the preparation of this volume for publication. The recent changes in the county's archaeological provision are alluded to in Graeme Bell's paper and in the final paper which also draws together some of the various issues raised throughout the volume.

Although for most of the county's history, neither the county's present boundaries nor those which existed before 1974 have much relevance to its past, nevertheless, they do provide the administrative framework within which current work is conducted. A constant refrain throughout the day was that work within the county was rarely driven by true research imperatives; in the last quarter of a century at least results have come from work which was essentially of a rescue nature, and was thus driven by the location of development rather than by selection according to research priorities. Further, there was a strong feeling that the application to the county's archaeology of the principles of competitive tendering has served only to fragment effort and knowledge, as well as introducing the use of criteria that are not in the best interests of quality of work and results.

For most of the periods into which archaeology and history are conventionally divided, the major problem consists of a lack of data, leading to the generation of hypotheses which are based upon a very small amount of information. This is shown to be true not just of prehistory and the 'Dark Ages', but also of the Roman period, too. Projects, such as the North West Wetlands Survey, offer the strongest opportunity to correct this, but the need is highlighted for substantial survey activity to be built into priorities; not only is it imperative from the point of view of working towards a more intelligible view of the county's past, but it also provides a vital tool for response-archaeology. Clearly, we cannot make a response to a development-threat (of whatever nature), until we know the potential of the area concerned. In some cases, it may be that the basic data does exist, but requires the attention of researchers to interpret it. For example, the aerial photographic evidence already amassed probably carries the potential to fill in some of the blank maps which speakers presented. Without this, we are going to make little progress in Lancashire in the important areas of cultural change and continuity. However, small projects such as that undertaken in the 1970s at Maiden Castle-on-Stainmore in advance of the re-alignment and improvement of the A66 road, demonstrate the potential clearly; here a small farmstead of the Romano-British period provides evidence of continuity stretching back to approximately 1000 BC and forward to the nineteenth century!

It is clear, sometimes as a result of accidental discoveries, that the area covered by Lancashire was not as inactive in prehistory as is sometimes supposed. Early prehistoric potential has been demonstrated by surveys such as that carried out in the 1970s on Anglezarke Moor, and, more comprehensive still, by the ongoing North West Wetlands Survey. Late prehistory is represented by dramatic sites such as the hillfort at Warton Crag, but how many of the farmstead sites assumed to be Romano-British have their origins at least in the late Iron Age, or indeed continued into the post-Roman period? Such possibilities may justify Nick Higham's reference to the Roman period as 'the Roman interlude'.

The Roman period itself appears at the first sight to have been better served; since the sixteenth century, a series of often-distinguished antiquarians have updated their observations. However, important though these are, the picture which they present is obviously weighted heavily in favour of the 'occupier', with little material available relating to the 'subject population' over three and a half centuries of occupation. Indeed, as shown above, current concerns emphasise a continuity of which the Roman period is a part; this was not as imperative for the antiquarians, impressed as they were by the monuments of a mighty empire, although some of their observations, albeit unwittingly, serve to illustrate several aspects of continuity. Their collected data, however, will help to provide the basis of research which will, as recently demonstrated at Gauber High Pasture in Upper Ribblesdale, open up long-term continuities.

The medieval period can be in part at least observed more easily; castles and ecclesiastical monuments survive to be subjected to modern recording techniques which, as at Lancaster Castle, can display the complexity of their use and development. Recorded and/or surviving sculptural remains offer their own clues to early medieval activity. Plenty of research remains to be done, however. Much more is needed on the transition from 'sub-Roman' to early medieval, where ecclesiastical monuments such as those at Heysham are of particular significance. Again, as recent work has suggested, long-term continuity may be of relevance at this site too. The motte-and-bailey sites of the Lune Valley, which take us back to Conquest times, have been little studied; and whilst Lancaster Castle may survive for the student, little is known in detail of the landscape that was dominated by it.

The Industrial Revolution may have been responsible for the destruction of much that proceeded it, though, as work at Manchester has indicated, it is possible to exaggerate this damage. In any case, it provided one of the substantial opportunities that was taken by antiquarians to report what was thereby revealed. Obviously townscapes were re-modelled under the influence of new wealth, as is potentially obvious if one examines the heart of a town such as Lancaster. It is therefore, ironical that the industrial and social revolutions of the second half of the twentieth century are doing much to destroy in their turn the evidence of the first revolution. Important work carried out by a number of organisations and individuals has helped to rescue information about this seminal period in the history of Lancashire; and in some cases the sites themselves are being preserved. Many more, however, particularly those distant from the main industrial centres, continue to rot away with only a minimal record of their existence. Such concerns do not end with the eighteenth and nineteenth centuries; after all, in the shadow of the fiftieth anniversary of V.E. Day, do we know all that we need of that important twentieth century monument, the air-raid shelter, or of military establishments which have remained secret until their dismantlement; the Royal Ordnance factory at Chorley is an example of this.

Work continues at varying paces in all of these areas; important, too, are the multi-period and multi-disciplinary approaches to the study of past environments in all of their aspects. It is clear that there are major projects, which are deserving of research funding. However, it is no use continuing to complain that the imperatives imposed by developer funding are not our imperatives. As we move into the twenty-first century, the most positive thought for the new millennium is that we have to make the developers' agenda our agenda.

To secure the greatest involvement from 'professionals' and 'amateurs' alike, we have to co-operate in the framing of research programmes that are geared to the work for which site-development provides the opportunity. In this way only can we maximise the available resources to take further the understanding of Lancashire's past.

1

THE HISTORY OF ARCHAEOLOGY IN LANCASHIRE

by Ben Edwards

I f proof were needed of Wheeler's maxim to the effect that archaeological information becomes knowledge only when it is published (Wheeler 1956, 209), the beginnings of archaeology in Lancashire provide it. If, for the present purpose, we define archaeology merely as a concern with the material remains of the past, it is clear that as far back as the period of place-naming in Old English, some people were aware of traces of earlier inhabitants. Thus places were given names with the *–chester* or *–caster* terminations which derive from Latin *castrum* and usually, though not invariably, denote a Roman fort or other settlement.

To suggest, however, that these originators of place-names were interested in their predecessors in the intellectual way in which modern archaeologists are interested in the past would be anachronistic. The medieval mind did not work in that way, and the passing acknowledgement of the existence of an earlier civilization is no more archaeology than the casual collection of a curious ancient artefact.

The antiquarian tradition

To meet men whose minds turned to the study of their fellows, past and present, we have to come to the period of the Renaissance, and in this country that effectively means the reign of Henry VIII. Not only was he himself in many ways a 'Renaissance Man', he had many such about him. Among them was John Leland, a young chaplain who had studied not only at both the English universities but at that of Paris as well, his earlier education at St Paul's School having been paid for by a rich benefactor.

Henry realised, or was reminded, at some stage after his decision to dissolve the monasteries had been taken, that the monastic libraries contained many treasures, and John Leland was appointed by a Commission under the Great Seal to visit them in order to search for English antiquities in 'all places where records, writings, and secrets of antiquity were deposited'. Cynicism suggests that cupidity rather than scholarship might have been Henry's motive, but it was Leland himself who petitioned Thomas Cromwell to extend his Commission to enable him to save manuscripts from destruction.

It will be observed that, whether or not Leland was formally 'King's Antiquary' as is sometimes said, his interests were wider than those of his master which were primarily documentary. Leland made copious notes during his journeys between 1534 and 1543 which were printed only in the eighteenth century (Hearne 1710), the *Dictionary of National Bibliography* somewhat sourly calling them 'a mass of undigested notes', which, of course, is precisely what they are. Leland planned, like so many others, a *magnum opus*, but perhaps another quotation from the *Dictionary of National Bibliography* may be a warning to us all. 'At length his antiquarian studies overtaxed his brain and he became incurably insane'.

His Lancashire notes are relatively few (Smith 1906–8), but some of them are of some interest. He described a house called Morley Hall, near Leigh at some length (*ibid*). The owner was Sir William Leland, and it has been speculated that the antiquary himself was a scion of this family. He noted at Manchester 'the dikes and fundations of Old Man Castel'. At Lancaster 'In thos partes in the feeldes and fundations hath ben found much Romayne coyne' and at Burrow (in Lonsdale) 'The plough menne find ther yn ering *lapides quadratos*, and many other straung things…' (*ibid*).

He also noted the presence of both carved stones and ancient coins at Ribchester, but did not mention the Romans. Instead he said 'Ther is a place wher that the people fable that the Jues had a temple' (*ibid*). This is an interesting piece of folklore and an example of a tendency to attribute ancient stonework to Jewish activity which must be based on an idea that Jews were frequently wealthy, and therefore more likely to be in possession of stone houses when others had to make do with wattle–and–daub. Leland's other passing comment that the tide ran in the Ribble up to half way between Preston and Ribchester (*ibid)*, was the first shot in the battle, still running, about whether or not the river was navigable as far as Ribchester in Roman times.

We have seen that Leland passed through Lancashire (probably more than once, his notes are widely scattered) observing things both contemporary and ancient. Whatever his intentions about writing a book, he was scarcely systematic. Half a century later we come to a man who was primarily interested in the past, who was systematic and who achieved his goal of writing what by any standards was a great book. This was William Camden, master of Westminster School and herald, ultimately Clarenceux King of Arms. While there might have been a little Lancashire blood in Leland's veins, Camden we can nearly claim as a native. In fact he was born in London, but his mother had been born a Curwen of that branch of the Workington family who lived at Poulton Hall, now lost in Morecambe.

Camden's *Britannia* was first published in 1586, in Latin, and was through five editions by the end of the century. It was first translated into English as the seventh edition of 1637. Camden accumulated his information by a combination of personal visits and the use of correspondents. He was in Lancashire in 1582 and again, specifically stated to be his second visit to Ribchester, in 1603. He almost certainly also passed through the county in 1599 when he toured the northern counties with Sir Robert Cotton. His Lancashire correspondents included his cousin's husband Thomas Braithwaite of Beaumont near Lancaster (Edwards 1994) and 'Limping' Thomas Talbot of Salesbury, Keeper of the Records in the Tower and a member of the Elizabethan Society of Antiquaries. He also used some notes passed to him by William Lambarde, jurist and historian of Kent. Lambarde had projected a similar volume to *Britannia*, and it can be speculated that he, in turn, had derived his information on a Ribchester inscription from the Nowell family of Read near Whalley. Earlier in his legal career Lambarde had been a pupil of a member of the Nowell family in their London law practice. There were also local archaeological correspondents at places like Ribchester at the beginning of the seventeenth century. Camden saw one of the Ribchester inscriptions 'in the house of Thomas Rhodes', and it was 'goodman Rhodes' who reported a stone which Braithwaite examined for Camden. Camden's *Britannia* remained the standard topographical history right through into the nineteenth century, being reissued under the editorship of Gibson in 1695 (reissued three times in the eighteenth century) and by Gough in 1789, reissued in 1806.

The flurry of activity at the beginning of the seventeenth century, occasioned largely by a desire to correct and amplify *Britannia*, was not maintained, and one can only presume that the troubled times leading to and succeeding the Civil War turned minds away from such peripheral matters as history. Not until the very end of the century do we hear of further interest in local antiquities. For example, the rev Thomas Machell, the 'Antiquary on Horseback' as Jane Ewbank christened him (Ewbank 1963), was riding round Cumberland and Westmorland in the last years of the century (Rogan and Birley 1955). Poor man, his plan of having his notes published for the benefit of his widow and children came to nothing, for Bishop Nicholson, in whose care they were left, rightly judged them unpublishable. He did, however, preserve them by adding them to the Chapter Library at Carlisle. Machell strayed into Lancashire far enough to record at Tunstall part of a tombstone from Burrow, of which a second portion remains there built into a barn and a third turned up in 1970 (Edwards 1971). Without Machell's record, it would have been almost impossible to make sense of the other two pieces.

Around the same time Charles Leigh must have been acquiring the information for his book published in 1700 under the imposing title of *The Natural History of Lancashire, Cheshire and the Peak, in Derbyshire, with an account of the British, Phoenician, Armenian, Greek and Roman antiquities in those parts*. Leigh, who hailed from Singleton Grange in the Fylde, took his BA at Oxford, left that city in debt and proceeded MA and MD at Cambridge. It is easy to scoff at the book's title, its complex apparatus of two Dedications, an Epistle to the Candid Reader, and a Preface, and even, as William Horsley was to do, at Leigh's ability to confuse two descriptions of the same Roman inscription. Nevertheless, Leigh deserves better. With its language modernised this couple of sentences could hang on the wall of any present–day archaeologist: 'To know what our Ancestors were, cannot be more lively delineated to us, than by the Ruines we discover of those Days; hence it is that by penetrating the Bowels of the Earth, we can trace the Footsteps of our Forefathers, and imprint upon our Minds some Idea's of their Times' (Leigh 1700, III, 1).

Although accused of 'vanity and petulance' by Whitaker, Leigh's healthy scepticism of received wisdom is shown by his refusal to believe in such contemporary myths as the generation of Barnacle Geese from shellfish, and he supported his argument against every natural historian from Aristotle on sound anatomical grounds (*ibid*, I, 158). So too, he refused to admit a Roman 'station' at Colne; on the grounds that although coins had been found there so they had elsewhere, but other evidence such as fortifications and inscriptions was lacking (*ibid*, III, 12). Some of his illustrations were better than some deemed acceptable nearly two centuries later.

Among Leigh's acquaintances was the rev Mr Ogden, the first incumbent of Ribchester who we know to have collected Roman material. We next hear of him in 1725 when that most famous of early antiquarians William Stukeley and his friend Roger Gale passed on their *Iter Boreale* (Stukeley 1776). They stayed about five hours in the neighbourhood of Ribchester, and were shown some of the local finds and sites before proceeding north to Lancaster. At Lancaster the travellers saw what they considered to be the remains of the wall of the Roman *castrum*, and noted 'All the space of ground north of the church is full of foundations of stone buildings, Roman, I believe'. Although the journey described in the *Iter Boreale* took place in 1725, the description of it was published only in the posthumous 2nd edition of *Itinerarium Curiosum* in 1776. In the meanwhile, elements of the archaeology of Lancashire had attracted the attention of other writers.

Of these, the most important was John Horsley, whose *Britannia Romana* was published in 1732. Horsley is, frankly, disappointing on Lancashire. True, he published the then known inscriptions, made disparaging remarks about Charles Leigh, and ventured some thoughts on the Roman roads of the county (Horsley 1732). Internal evidence, however, suggests that, on the latter particularly, he relied on correspondence rather than personal inspection. At Chester, incidentally, one of his informants was a Mr

Prescott, who was the son of the Mr Prescott to whom the widow of Mr Ogden of Ribchester had passed his collection. The Prescott family dwelt at Ayrefield, Upholland, and evidently brought a Chester Mithraic figure back to their home, where it was rediscovered in the 1960s to cause confusion for some time until its real origin was recognised (Edwards 1977).

With the exception of Leigh, practically everyone considered thus far has been a national figure. We now turn to another local product. The rev Richard Rauthmell was born at the end of the seventeenth century, just over the historical county border, in Bowland (Edwards 1967, 241). At Cambridge, he made the acquaintance of Robert Fenwick of Burrow-in-Lonsdale who was to build a new house on the site of the Roman fort there. This was still identified as *Bremetennacum*, and, as a result, the book which Rauthmell wrote about the site was entitled *Antiquitates Bremetonnacenses* (Rauthmell 1746). There is no doubt that Rauthmell was an enthusiast, and that enthusiasm sometimes led him astray. Nevertheless, he did better than might be thought from Eric Birley's remark that 'Seldom can so large a book have been written from so little material' (Birley 1946, 131). Whitaker, too, was dismissive if gentler, but it must be said that some of the errors in the published book can be attributed to the printer, as can be seen from an examination of the manuscript, which is in the Harris Museum, Preston. That volume, incidentally, was given by the author to Thomas Lister Parker of Browsholme, his Bowland patron.

Towards the end of the eighteenth century, we begin to get a flurry of books relating to the past of the county. The rev John Whitaker published the first volume of his *History of Manchester* in 1771. Whitaker's *Manchester* had a much wider remit than its title would suggest, covering the region, as we would now call it (Whitaker 1771). Thomas Pennant journeyed through the county recording antiquities, allegedly in 1773 (Pennant 1801). Pennant, from Holywell in Flintshire, is perhaps best known as one of Gilbert White's correspondents for the *Natural History of Selborne*. He published a number of 'Tours', however, and that through Lancashire was published posthumously in 1801. It is specifically stated to have taken place in 1773, but the doubt arises from the description of Ribchester Bridge, which had been washed away in 1771 and not replaced until 1776 (Edwards 1994).

Most of what had been recorded of the archaeology of Lancashire up to this time was, of course, of Roman and post-Roman date. Few people could conceive, for both cultural and religious reasons, of a lengthy antiquity for man. Stukeley and others had recorded what we now know to be prehistoric monuments and artefacts, though not in Lancashire, but they were all assigned to a vague set of 'Ancient Britons'. Now, too, some prehistoric artefacts begin to be recorded from Lancashire. Among the first were part of an Iron Age sword and its scabbard from Warton near Carnforth (Garstang 1906, 247; Newman 1996, 15).

ROMAN BRONZE HELMET, FOUND AT RIBCHESTER.

The Ribchester helmet found in 1796
(from W T Watkin, 1883, Roman Lancashire)

Right at the end of the century, however, we have the discovery of the two most important individual Roman objects from the county — the Ribchester helmet and the Kirkham shield boss. The former was found by thirteen-year-old James Walton in 1796 (Edwards 1992). It was bought, together with most of the associated objects, by Charles Townley, at the instigation of Thomas Dunham Whitaker (*ibid*). The Kirkham shield-boss, the first intimation recorded of the possible existence there of a Roman site, was found by John Willacy, delightfully described as 'an old, dissipated and eccentric schoolmaster' (Ronson 1851, 10). It was sold by him to Dr Hunter of York, and came eventually, like the Ribchester helmet, to Townley.

The nineteenth century

Moving onto the nineteenth century interest in the past increased both locally and nationally. It starts, of course, with the greatest of Lancashire's topographical historians, Thomas Dunham Whitaker, of Holme in Cliviger. The spirit of his books belongs to the eighteenth century tradition. *An History of Whalley* first appeared in 1801, and *An History of Richmondshire* not until 1823–5, the former including, by editorial sleight of hand, Ribchester, the latter Burrow-in-Lonsdale. However dated in concept these volumes may have been, their author was not. He collected prehistoric objects like the Bronze Age flat axes from Read and a gold torque from his own land at Cliviger. Moreover, he instigated the first deliberate archaeological excavation of which I can find record in the county, when he investigated part of the Roman fort site at Ribchester, discovering one of its most important inscriptions. Even more

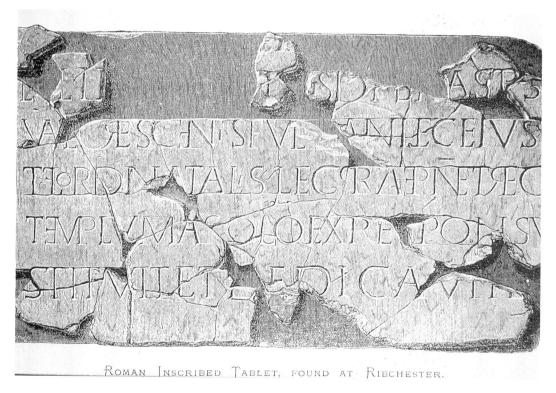

ROMAN INSCRIBED TABLET, FOUND AT RIBCHESTER.

Roman inscription from Ribchester, reported by T D Whitaker; as found by workmen in 1811 (from W T Watkin, 1883, Roman Lancashire)

importantly, he collected all the available Roman inscriptions from the site, and bequeathed them to his College, St John's at Cambridge (now loaned by the Master and Fellows to Ribchester Museum).

By the middle of the nineteenth century the first of the two county societies had been founded, the Historic Society of Lancashire and Cheshire. The distribution of wealth and influence in the county, however, dictated that it was based not in the historic county centres like Lancaster or Preston but in Liverpool, and covered, as its name tells us, the neighbouring county as well. By 1863 the Cumberland and Westmorland Antiquarian and Archaeological Society had been formed, and, from the beginning included Lancashire-North-of-Sands in its territory. Finally, in 1883, Manchester followed where Liverpool had led, and the Lancashire and Cheshire Antiquarian Society was formed. The effect of this curious relationship of the county to its archaeological societies is not capable of precise assessment, but was probably considerable on the subsequent development of the subject in the county.

Of those who contributed to the volumes of the Historic Society as the century proceeded, we need mention only the occasional name. Joseph Mayer, collector, of Liverpool was the Society's first curator. John Just specialised in Roman roads, and the rev William Thornber of Blackpool contributed several papers which have been much mistrusted, but are too often judged by the standards of the present rather than those of his own day. Whoever contributed, some of the illustrations from early volumes show how wide was the interest of the society's members, often in what we might think of as fairly 'modern' subjects, for example half timbered buildings, medieval pottery, and clay tobacco pipes. Towards the end of the century people like Dr Henry Colley March were discoursing on such widely-varying themes as flints found on the high moors, the 'Roman' road over Blackstone Edge, and the Halton cross (March 1883; March 1891).

Another name which occurs in the 1870s is that of W Thompson Watkin, and all his knowledge of the Romans in the county was collected in the volume entitled *Roman Lancashire*, published in 1883. Also in the late nineteenth century papers on pre-Conquest sculpture were produced by both Bishop George Browne and J Romilly Allen, the first evidence of interest in the subject in the county (Browne 1887; Allen 1893).

After Whitaker's initial foray in 1812, little excavation work had been carried out at Ribchester, with the exception of the exposure of a fragment of the fort wall for the delectation of delegates to the 1850 Archaeological Congress held in Manchester and Lancaster (Just and Harland 1851). In 1883 several small trenches were opened (Smith and Shortt 1890). At the end of the century, however, excavations were undertaken which led to the putting of Ribchester, so to say 'on the archaeological map'. These

*Aerial photograph of Ribchester, one of the first sites in Lancashire
to attract the attention of antiquarians*

were carried out by John Garstang, later to become Professor of Egyptology at Liverpool University. In 1898, however, he was an undergraduate son of a Blackburn doctor reading mathematics at Oxford. His interest in this subject marched well with an interest in astronomy, and it seems that his journeyings from Blackburn to the observatory at Stonyhurst College drew his attention to the Roman site at Ribchester. Discussion of this back at Oxford with the Camden Professor of Ancient History, Francis Haverfield, led to the suggestion of excavation. Garstang's efforts were not his greatest work in archaeology, but they determined his career and maintained interest in the Roman site (Garstang 1898). This was important when, a few years later, conversion work to turn a group of cottages near the river was the stimulus for what must be still one of the odder pieces of Roman archaeology in this country. Miss Margaret Greenall, for whom the conversion was taking place, was a member of the brewing family of Greenall at Warrington. Their Wilderspool brewery was on the Roman site there, a site which had been investigated for several years by an Inland Revenue official named Thomas May who was now brought to Ribchester by Miss

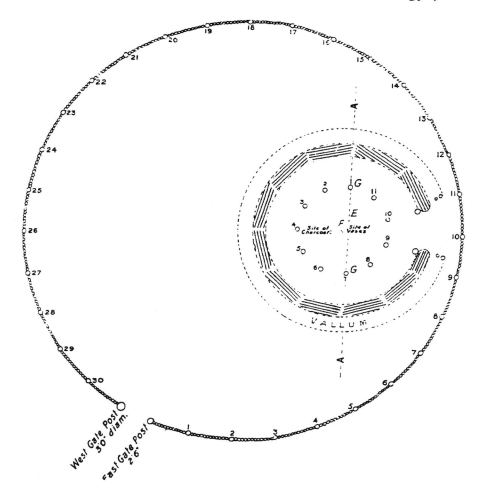

Bleasdale Circle, as surveyed by Sydney Wilson in 1900

Greenall and excavated within the cottages as they were converted, recovering much of the plan of the *principia* of the stone fort. May's work led to the setting up of the site museum at Ribchester.

Aside from Roman archaeology, the nineteenth century witnessed the most improbable and unbalancing find ever made in the county, and the one which has the greatest significance outside its bounds. That was, of course, the discovery, on 15 May, 1840, of the Cuerdale Hoard (Philpott 1990). That massive hoard of coins and hacksilver, deposited by the banks of the Ribble about 903 AD, remains not merely the heaviest Viking silver hoard in Europe but is many times heavier than its nearest rival. Its implications, with the majority of its coins apparently arriving from the east while the silver seems to have travelled east, are still by no means clear. Sadly, we shall never know its full contents, Treasure Trove practice being so different in the nineteenth century from that of the present day. To say that all concerned with the Norse immigrations to Britain await Professor James Graham-Campbell's full account of the hoard with impatience, is to understate the case.

The development of modern archaeology

With the twentieth century I shall deal summarily. Like Caesar's Gaul, it comes in three parts; down to the end of World War I; to the end of World War II; and the subsequent fifty years to the present. As has already been hinted, the earliest of the three periods was in many ways an extension of the nineteenth century. By 1915 Ribchester Museum was opened, and by the end of the war Lancaster Priory church had acquired its new north aisle, involving the demolition of the old north wall yielding its haul of pre-Conquest sculpture (Taylor 1906). Between the wars, Droop excavated in Lancaster (Droop and Newstead 1928, 1929, 1930). The excavation of the Bleasdale monument, first discovered at the beginning of the century (Dawkins 1900), marked the first use of pollen analysis on a Lancashire site (Varley 1938). As for the last fifty years, we are, of course, too close to the wood to select the right trees for comment. Pickering took up the challenges of Walton-le-Dale (Pickering 1957) and Kirkham (unfortunately never published). Under-resourced, it was not his fault that his results were less clear than they might have been. Yet who is to say that the recent excavations on both sites by the Lancaster University Archaeological Unit would have taken place with only the nineteenth century evidence to justify them. So too, Professor Richmond at Lancaster made the best bricks he could with the clay and straw in his hands (Richmond 1953). Lancaster was his last excavation, and I treasure the memory of sitting chatting to him in the sun on the bank of the Vicarage garden.

If that has introduced a personal note it is intentional. Over the last thirty years I have observed a vast change come over the archaeology of the county. I came as the country's first general County Archaeologist. I ranged for ten years from Barrow-in-Furness to south Manchester. Sometimes frustrated, usually fulfilled, I have added a few crumbs to the total of knowledge about the county's archaeology. Then came, not all together, the change in the size and shape of the county, the setting up by Adrian Olivier of the Sites and Monuments Record, the creation of the Unit, and the change in the nature of the role of later appointed County Archaeologists. Today I see a scene in which those without formal qualifications find it more difficult to make a real contribution to archaeological knowledge. At the same time, I observe the recovery of a much greater proportion of the finite resource which is archaeological information in the earth. That scene which I have just outlined, I view with mixed feelings. I look to the future with similar feelings. I see an archaeological future for the county of which I shall be an observer, for by the summer I shall have retired and I shall not have an immediate successor [1]. I can say only that I hope all those into whose hands various parts of Lancashire's archaeological heritage are trusted in the future, as part has been to mine, get as much enjoyment out of that trust as I have.

[1]. *This paper was compiled in 1995 before the initiation of the changes discussed in the final two papers in this volume.*

References

Allen, J Romilly, 1893 The early christian monuments of Lancashire, *Trans Hist Soc Lancashire Cheshire*, **45**, 1–45

Birley, E B, 1946 The Roman fort at Burrow-in-Lonsdale, *Trans Cumberland Westmorland Antiq Archaeol Soc*, N Ser **46**, 126–156

Browne, G F, 1887 Pre-Norman stones in Lancashire, *Trans Lancashire Cheshire Antiq Soc*, **5**, 1–18

Camden, W, 1586 *Britannia*, London

Dawkins, W B, 1900 On the exploration of prehistoric sepulchral remains of the Bronze Age at Bleasdale by S Jackson, Esq, *Trans Lancashire Cheshire Antiq Soc* **18**, 114–124

Droop, J P, and Newstead, R, 1928 Trial excavations at Lancaster, *Liverpool Ann Archaeol Anth*, **15**, 33–40

Droop, J P, and Newstead, R, 1929 Excavations at Lancaster, *Liverpool Ann Archaeol Anth*, **16**, 25–36

Droop, J P, and Newstead, R, 1930 Excavations at Lancaster, 1929, *Liverpool Ann Archaeol Anth*, **17**, 57–72

Edwards, B J N, 1994 Thomas Braithwaite of Beaumont and William Camden, *Contrebis*, **19**, 1–13

Edwards, B J N, 1971 Roman finds from *Contrebis*, *Trans Cumberland Westmorland Antiq Archaeol Soc*, N Ser, **71**, 17-34

Edwards, B J N, 1977 A Chester Mithraic figure restored?, *Chester Archaeol Journ*, **60**, 56–60

Edwards, B J N, 1967 Richard Rauthmell, *Trans Cumberland Westmorland Antiq Archaeol Soc*, N Ser, **67**, 241

Edwards, B J N, 1994 How did Thomas Pennant cross the Ribble?, *Lancashire Local Historian*, **9**, 8–11

Edwards, B J N, 1992 *The Ribchester Hoard*, Preston

Ewbank, J M, 1963 *Antiquary on Horseback*, Trans Cumberland Westmorland Antiq Archaeol Soc, Extra Ser, **19**, Kendal

Garstang, J, 1898 *Roman Ribchester*, Preston, London, and Oxford

Garstang, J, 1906 Early Man, in *The Victoria History of the County of Lancaster* (eds W Farrer and J Brownbill), London, **1**, 211-256

Graham Campbell, J, forthcoming *The Cuerdale Hoard and related Viking Age silver from Britain and Ireland in the British Museum*

Hearne, T, (ed) 1710 *The itinerary of John Leland the antiquary*, Oxford

Horsley, J, 1732 *Britannia Romana*, London

Just, J, and Harland, J, 1851 On Roman Ribchester, *Journ British Archaeol Assoc*, **6**, 229–251

Leigh, C, 1700 *The Natural History of Lancashire, Cheshire and the Peak in Derbyshire*, Oxford

March, H C, 1883 The road over Blackstone Edge, *Trans Lancashire and Cheshire Antiq Soc*, **1**, 73–86

March, H C, 1891 The pagan christian overlap in the North, *Trans Lancashire Cheshire Antiq Soc*, **9**, 49–89

Newman, R, 1996 Warton Crag Hill–fort, *Keer to Kent*, **29**, 14–15

Pennant, T, 1801 *A Tour from Downing to Alston Moor*, London

Philpott, F A, 1990 *A Silver saga*, Liverpool

Pickering, E E, 1957 Roman Walton-le-Dale, *Trans Hist Soc Lancashire Cheshire*, **109**, 1–46

Rauthmell, R, 1746 *Antiquitates Bremetonacenses*, Kirkby Lonsdale

Richmond I A, 1953 Excavations on the site of the Roman fort at Lancaster, *Trans Hist Soc Lancashire Cheshire*, **105**, 1–23

Rogan, J, and Birley, E B, 1955 Thomas Machell the Antiquary, *Trans Cumberland Westmorland Antiq Archaeol Soc*, N ser, **55**, 132–153

Ronson, J, 1851 Notes on the seventh *Iter* of Richard of Cirencester, *Trans Hist Soc Lancashire Cheshire*, **3**, 10

Smith, T C, and Shortt, J, 1890 *The history of the parish of Ribchester*, London and Preston

Smith, L, Toulmin (ed) 1906–8 *Leland's Itinerary*, v **2, 4, 5**

Stukeley, W, 1776 *Itinerarium Curiosum*, 2nd ed, London

Taylor, H, 1906 *The ancient crosses and holy wells of Lancashire*, Manchester

Varley, W J, 1938 The Bleasdale Circle, *Antiq Journ*, **18**, 154–171

Watkin, W T, 1883 *Roman Lancashire*, Liverpool

Wheeler, R E M, 1956 *Archaeology from the earth*, Oxford

Whitaker, J, 1771 *The history of Manchester*, **1**, Manchester

Whitaker, T D, 1801 *An history of Whalley*, London

Whitaker, T D, 1823–5 *An history of Richmondshire*, London

2

THE UPPER PALAEOLITHIC
AND MESOLITHIC

by Ron Cowell

Even where evidence is relatively plentiful, archaeological patterns contained within the boundaries of a modern county often will provide only an incomplete understanding of the way in which ancient social and economic forces operated. This is particularly true for the period of the Mesolithic hunter-gatherers, as a high degree of mobility is generally thought to be the defining criterion for the resulting settlement and landuse pattern. The importance of the archaeology of Mesolithic Lancashire can only be recognised if the present, relatively limited, amount of evidence is understood in the context of wider patterns of Mesolithic settlement and landuse. In order to understand the significance of the material found within the present boundaries of Lancashire, the definition of the county has been extended to include its historic area. This allows the more plentiful material from Merseyside and Greater Manchester to be included. Some better investigated upland sites that lie just within Yorkshire, have also been included as comparative material for the discussion of the Lancashire evidence.

This wider study area allows for the potential recognition of prehistoric patterns that will serve to guide future research. It contains landscapes associated with the coastal fringe, coastal and inland mosslands, major river valleys and estuaries, a range of lowland soil types, and medium and high uplands that potentially make it of national importance in identifying the full range of hunter-gatherer adaptations to the landscape.

The Upper Palaeolithic

The earliest hunter-gatherer evidence for the county relates to the end of the last (Devensian) Ice Age, during the late Upper Palaeolithic (*c* 16,000–8000 BC). This evidence is sparse, as the ice has done much to obliterate and cover earlier landscapes and the sites that must have once existed, so no meaningful pattern of occupation

Palaeolithic sites in or near Lancashire

can be reconstructed. Northern Lancashire is the most important area with three sites. Two cave sites are known on the northern side of Morecambe Bay; Kirkhead cave (now in Cumbria) has produced artefacts of this period and disputed stratigraphic evidence which dates the occupation to 8700 ± 200 BC (Ashmead *et al* 1974; Gale and Hunt 1985, 1990; Salisbury 1986; Tipping 1986), while to the north-east at the mouth of the River Kent three Upper Palaeolithic blades have come from Lindale Low (Salisbury 1988). To the south at Poulton-le-Fylde, the remains of an elk, with associated barbed points, provided a radiocarbon date of 10,400 ± 300 BC (Hallam et al 1973; Jacobi et al 1986), although the date may need revision (Middleton *et al* 1995, 87). These sites date from the period near the end of the Devensian, during the general trend to warming as the ice cap retreated northwards.

The nature of the Mesolithic evidence

The evidence for the period after *c* 8000 BC is however much stronger in the county and has been traditionally biased to the central Pennine uplands, where collectors have over the last hundred years or so located scatters of struck flint eroding from under thin peats (*eg* Jacobi *et al* 1976; Stonehouse 1989, 1994). This has produced the greatest concentration of Mesolithic sites in the country, although the number of sites within the Lancashire Pennines is small in comparison with those from the adjacent areas of Yorkshire (Wymer and Bonsall 1977).

Most sites in the uplands are represented by surface assemblages, ranging from a few pieces of struck flint to several thousand, which are found either in small restricted areas or spread more evenly across the landscape (Stonehouse 1989). They are situated mainly between the 366m and 488m contours (Jacobi *et al* 1976), with the greatest concentration being found in a fairly restricted area between Saddleworth and Marsden, where the Pennines are at their narrowest. The western edge of this distribution overlaps into Lancashire. Areas immediately to the north and south of this narrow watershed, have been reportedly searched by collectors but comparative densities do not occur (Stonehouse 1989, 1994). Further to the north, the Pennines are almost devoid of sites, but since this area does not have a similar history of flint collection it is not clear to what extent this reflects the true archaeological distribution.

This evidence from the high uplands, however, represents only one facet of the exploitation of the landscape of the North West, as contemporary remains are also found in the lowlands. Here, evidence has been slower to emerge and has resulted largely from systematic fieldwork since the early 1980s. This has been mainly undertaken by the National Museums and Galleries on Merseyside and the North West Wetland Survey, a project managed through LUAU.

		Early
▲		Late
△		Unknown

Land over 200m   Lowland peat

Mesolithic sites in or near Lancashire

The strongest evidence presently lies in the southern part of the historic county, now Merseyside. The coastal and estuarine areas have provided the densest scatters of surface flintwork, particularly around the lower reaches of the river Alt near Little Crosby, which is mirrored to a lesser extent on the adjacent north Wirral coast just outside the study area (Cowell and Innes 1994).

Inland, the lowland archaeological distribution becomes sparser the farther east one goes, although there are some indications that larger concentrations do exist, particularly around mosslands as at Chat Moss in Greater Manchester (Hall *et al* 1995) and Mawdesley in West Lancashire (G Stephens pers comm), or in river valleys as at Marle's Wood in the Ribble valley (Middleton 1993). Much of the inland evidence often consists of only one or two struck flint pieces (Cowell 1991; Cowell and Innes 1994).

To the north of the Ribble, fieldwork has so far provided a similar pattern on inland soils with only occasional very small sites found. A concentration of material in a valley site at Halton in north Lancashire is the main exception (Penney 1978). Coastal material is not as frequent as further to the south in Merseyside, but does include two potentially important sites at Heysham Head (Salisbury and Sheppard 1994) and Peel, near Lytham (Middleton 1993; Middleton *et al* 1995).

This archaeology exists alongside a body of palaeoecological evidence. Work on the vegetational history of the uplands suggests that the woodland was being extensively affected by fire at this time (Jacobi *et al* 1976), which may represent human manipulation of the animal resources and their habitats (Mellars 1976). Palynological studies show that during the later Mesolithic in the lowlands small episodes of woodland reduction can be identified at a number of sites, which may reflect human manipulation of the vegetation. Inland, these woodland reduction episodes are infrequent at individual sites, small scale, and separated by long periods of dense woodland regeneration. As in the uplands, however, many of the inland peat bogs show extensive evidence of burning in likely Mesolithic levels (Cowell and Innes 1994; Middleton *et al* 1995), which if caused by people is associated with subsistence activities that leave little trace in the archaeological record. In the coastal areas, woodland reduction episodes are a little more common at individual sites, and surrounding vegetation cover is generally lighter (Cowell and Innes 1994).

The local pollen evidence includes four sites in the area where cereal-type pollen is found associated with tree reduction episodes of Mesolithic date, just after *c* 4000 cal BC (Cowell and Innes 1994; Tooley 1978; Williams 1985), many centuries before cultural material associated with the first farmers of the Neolithic is found in Britain. This may represent the first evidence for the beginning of the slow, gradual, and complex process of the move from hunter-gathering to the adoption of agriculture.

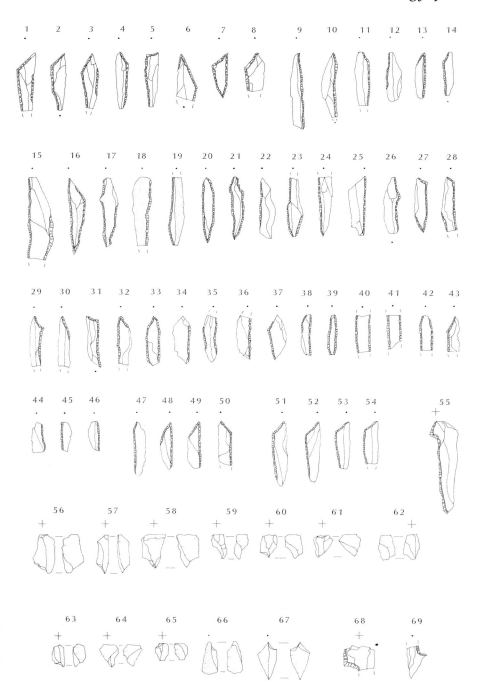

Late Mesolithic microlith production from Piethorn Brook, Milnrow, Lancashire
(after Poole 1986)

Excavated sites

More excavation has taken place on upland sites than in the lowlands, largely through the work of Buckley before the war (Barnes 1982). Some of this work has been limited in scope and has not been published accessibly. The main upland Lancashire sites to have been more recently excavated lie near Milnrow (Poole 1986) and at Anglezarke (Howard-Davies and Quartermaine forthcoming). Some understanding of the upland sites is, however, possible from excavations on Pennine sites mainly in Yorkshire (Radley and Mellars 1964; Stonehouse 1986; and summarised in Barnes 1982). These sites generally are represented by circular arrangements of struck flint over small areas of *c* 15–20 m^2, often with hearths or evidence of burning and the occasional site has structural evidence in the form of small stake holes, circular arrangements of stone or possible paved areas.

This work in the uplands has produced a basic chronology for the Mesolithic in the North which has been applied to changing flint technology, particularly of microliths

Windy Hill area, near Milnrow, in the Pennines

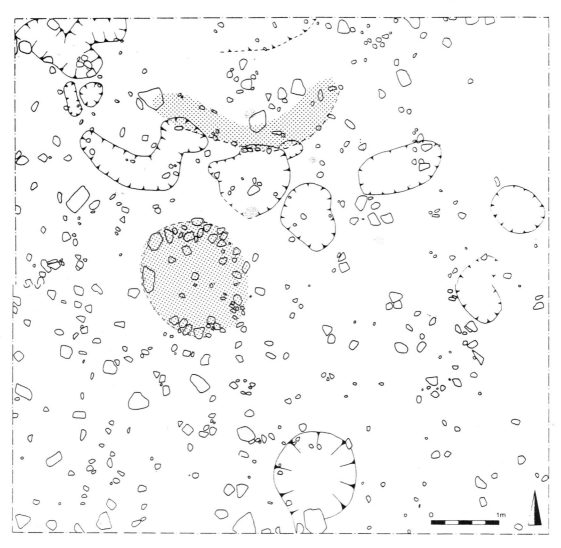

Trench plan from Rushy Brow, Anglezarke; the shading highlights two empheral structures

(which may have represented arrowheads or armatures for hunting). This suggests that there is a distinctive flint technology for sites of the early Mesolithic dated *c*7500–6800 cal BC based on 'broad blade' characteristics and another, 'geometric' style for the subsequent later Mesolithic up to *c* 3800 cal BC or possibly a little later (Jacobi 1976, 1987; Mellars 1976b). This broad division appears to hold, although many of the particular dates are less useful as they often have wide deviations and the contexts of the dated material is not always secure (Jacobi 1987).

Excavation of a lowland Mesolithic site at Croxteth Park, Liverpool

The only dating evidence for the lowlands in the North West comes from excavations at sites north of Lancashire, at Williamson's Moss and Eskmeals in the Cumbrian plain (Bonsall 1981; Bonsall *et al* 1986). Little extensive excavation has taken place in the Lancashire lowlands, but includes river valley sites at Croxteth Park and three in the Ditton Brook valley in Merseyside (Cowell in prep), Marle's Wood, Ribchester (J Hallam pers comm), and the coastal location of Heysham Head (Salisbury and Shepperd 1994). An important moss edge site in West Lancashire at Mawdesley has also been partially excavated (G Stephens pers comm). Little of this work has been published but the range of evidence from the sites is known to be limited, being restricted to distribution plots of flintwork of varying thoroughness. The only recorded structural evidence, a small hollow with a double stake-hole next to it, comes from Ditton Brook 1. No dating material has come from any of these excavations. As microlith-rich surface sites are also very rare in the lowlands, dating by typological comparison with upland flint assemblages is also not possible for the vast majority of lowland sites. Attribution to the later Mesolithic, therefore, has to be more tentative for many of these sites. The flint assemblages from the above sites do include a small microlithic element, and certain associated technological and raw material traits allow some grounds for tentatively assigning a proportion of surface sites to the later Mesolithic (Cowell and Innes 1994, Middleton *et al* 1995).

In conclusion, as far as chronology is concerned, sites of the early Mesolithic are largely confined to areas outside the study area, most notably the Yorkshire Pennines (Jacobi 1978) and the lowlands of the Wirral (Cowell 1992), although the site at Anglezarke dates to this period (Howard-Davies and Quartermaine forthcoming). Other evidence may be represented in the lowlands, around the Alt estuary in Merseyside (Cowell and Innes 1994) and in the Irwell valley, Greater Manchester (Spencer 1951). The number of sites increase in the late Mesolithic with the greatest concentration being found in the Pennines (Barnes 1982), while many of the small lowland sites have largely been assigned to this period (Cowell and Innes 1994).

Interpreting surface scatters

No faunal, pollen, or botanical evidence has come from any of the excavated sites so that site function has largely to be interpreted from lithic analysis and ethnographic comparison. The tree reduction and evidence of burning in the uplands suggests that the woodlands were being managed to some extent to attract herbivores (Mellars 1976a). Most of the upland flint assemblages are dominated by microliths, implying hunting was an important part of the activities at such sites, while domestic activities may have been more limited. By implication these sites are held to represent summer hunting camps, occupied by a limited number of people (Mellars 1976b), although it is not clear how the larger agglomerations of surface material fit into this pattern, unless the same camps were used each year. Williams (1985) argues on the basis of vegetational changes from pollen evidence at Soyland Moor, Yorkshire, for an intensive form of managed grazing over many centuries in parts of the Pennines. This would have required a greater degree of settlement permanence than is envisaged by the current interpretation of the archaeological evidence.

Interpretation of the lowland evidence is less agreed, as it has to proceed largely from small flint assemblages from surface sites. Sites outside the study area, on the Cumbrian plain have the largest flint assemblages in the lowlands of the North West (Bonsall 1981; Bonsall *et al* 1986) and differ markedly from assemblages from the Lancashire lowlands (Cowell and Innes 1994; Middleton *et al* 1995) having a higher percentage of microliths. This indicates that many of the Lancashire lowland sites at least appear to differ in function from the upland sites. The lithic evidence suggests that the lowlands might include both base camps and smaller specialised sites (Cowell and Innes 1994; Middleton *et al* 1995). The base camps were probably mainly in coastal areas, where larger groups may have congregated for longer periods of time, possibly in the winter (Bonsall 1981, 1986). The specialised smaller sites, may have included kill sites, butchery sites, hunting stands, bivouac sites etc (Price 1978). Small-scale

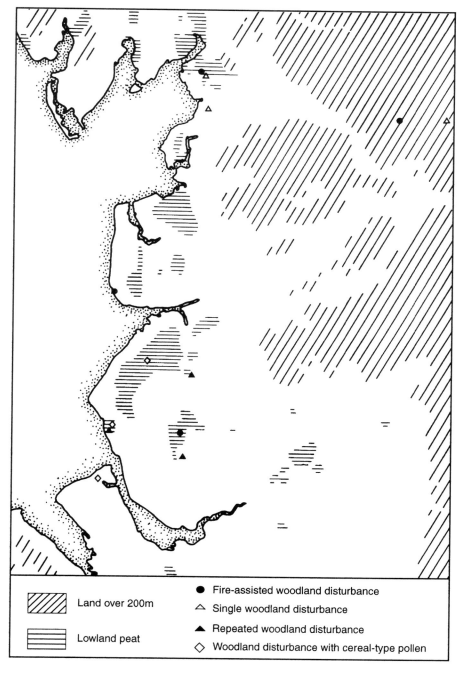

Distribution of pollen sites with Mesolithic woodland disturbances
in or near Lancashire (after Zvelebil 1994, with additions)

manipulation of the woodlands was also taking place in the lowlands, sometimes associated with evidence of burning suggesting fire-induced woodland clearance.

In the early Mesolithic in eastern Yorkshire and Lincolnshire (Jacobi 1978) and on the Wirral (Cowell 1992), the occurrence of flint and chert tools, many miles from the stone sources, suggests the movement of people and goods and provides the possibility of identifying the economic patterns behind this mobility. In the late Mesolithic such patterns are harder to identify, although little attempt has thus far been made to compare raw material use across the county. Preliminary indications from published sources imply that different raw materials are used north and south of the Ribble, with areas to the north using a greater range of materials, most notably including various chert types, probably from the Pennines (Cowell and Innes 1994; Middleton *et al* 1995). It may be that raw material exploitation and subsequent use is carried out on a much smaller, more local scale during the late Mesolithic in the region.

The national and local importance of the evidence

The late Upper Palaeolithic material from Lancashire is limited, but it is the earliest evidence for settlement this far north and as such is nationally important. Material elsewhere in northern England is rare for this period, with only two cave sites in the Yorkshire Pennines providing similarly limited evidence. The main sites for this period are found in the southern part of Britain with the exception of an important number of cave sites in Derbyshire (Jacobi 1980).

The potential of Mesolithic evidence from North West England is amongst the best in the country with its large number of upland sites, an increasing number of lowland sites adjacent to wet mire, alluvial, and coastal deposits, and a body of detailed pollen studies for both upland and lowland. This provides a range of potentially associated evidence that is present in only a few areas of the country. Investigating across the full range of environments present in Lancashire could lead to a better understanding of the nature of Mesolithic social and economic patterns in the region that would be of national significance.

The pollen evidence from some Lancashire sites also suggests that there may be potential for investigating the transition period from hunter gathering to farming in the region. This is a period where evidence is scanty everywhere and interpretation open to many difficulties (Zvelebil 1986, 1994). The increasing number of coastal sites provides Lancashire with archaeological evidence potentially as important as that in Cumbria, where an argument has been put forward for a less mobile system that may have facilitated the earlier adoption of agriculture in such favoured areas (Bonsall 1981).

The location of sites in Lancashire has benefitted from systematic survey, particularly in the lowlands, so that the distributional pattern for the county is constantly improving. The quality of investigation and interpretation of this material is very limited, however, and compares poorly with adjacent areas of the Pennines and flanking lowlands to the east. Analysis of the surface material needs to be improved so that some broad patterns of landscape exploitation can be outlined on a par with studies of later prehistoric surface material for parts of southern England (*eg* Schofield 1991). The lack of excavated sites restricts understanding of the dating of much material, while the lack of structural, faunal, or environmental evidence from those that have been excavated makes interpretation of the evidence difficult.

The research agenda

In order to develop the potential of the Lancashire evidence the following steps should be taken:

- systematic field survey sampling needs to continue across the region to provide a representative surface pattern across the whole county, including less well researched areas such as the lowlands away from the coasts and mosslands, and the northern Pennines (current landuse permitting);

- a larger number of representative sites, particularly in the lowlands, where the range of site types may be greater, needs to be excavated, allowing a better understanding of the range of site types and function present in the region through lithic and structural analysis;

- additionally palaeoecological studies, in concert with site-specific investigations, may allow the degree of seasonality and economic mobility to be gauged from faunal and vegetational evidence;

- incorporating raw material studies into flint technology analysis may lead to the recognition of patterns of lithic procurement, use, and disposal across large areas, with implications for the identification of social, economic and territorial patterns in the region;

- a better definition of the chronology and associated flint technology of the periods would aid the understanding of the transition to farming and allow more of the small surface material sites, by which the Mesolithic is mainly recognised in the lowlands, to be assigned more securely to the period;

- localised, detailed patterns of sea level change need to be developed alongside site analysis in present coastal locations, so that the nature of Mesolithic coastal exploitation and the potential for sedentary settlement patterns can be better understood.

Priority should be given to those sites where waterlogged deposits are most likely to be present which include coastal and intertidal environments, lowland mires, alluvial deposits, and upland blanket peat, but even dryland sites in a range of environments should be evaluated to test for survival of relevant evidence.

References

Ashmead, R M, Ashmead, P, and Wood, R H, 1974 Second report on the archaeological excavations at Kirkhead Cavern, *North West Speleology*, **2(1)**, 24–33

Barnes, B, 1982 *Man and the changing landscape*, Merseyside County Council/Merseyside County Museums/ University of Liverpool, Work Notes **3**, Liverpool

Bonsall, C, 1980 The coastal factor in the Mesolithic settlement of North West England, in *The Mesolithic in Europe* (ed B Gramsch), Veröffentlichungen des Museums für Ur- and Frühgeschichte, Potsdam, **14/15**, 451–472

Bonsall, C, Sunderland, D, Tipping, R, and Cherry, J, 1986 The Eskmeals Project 1981–5: an interim report, *Northern Archaeol*, **7(1)**, 1–30

Cowell, R W, 1991 The prehistory of Merseyside, *Journ Merseyside Archaeol Soc*, **7**, 21–61

Cowell, R W, 1992 Greasby, North Wirral. Excavations at an early Mesolithic site: interim report, *Archaeol North West*, **4**, 7–15

Cowell, R W, in prep *Excavations on three Mesolithic sites in Merseyside and their place in the Mesolithic of North West England*

Cowell, R W, and Innes, J B, 1994 *The wetlands of Merseyside*, North West Wetlands Survey, **1**, Lancaster Imprints, **2**, Lancaster

Gale, S J, and Hunt, C O, 1985 The stratigraphy of Kirkhead Cave, an upper Palaeolithic site in Northern England, *Proc Prehist Soc*, **51**, 283–304

Gale, S J, and Hunt, C O, 1990 The stratigraphy of Kirkhead Cave, an upper Palaeolithic site in Northern England: discussion, *Proc Prehist Soc*, **56**, 51–56

Hall, D, Wells, C, Huckerby, E, Meyer, A, and Cox, C, 1995 *The wetlands of Greater Manchester*, North West Wetlands Survey, **2**, Lancaster Imprints, **3**, Lancaster

Hallam, J S, Edwards, B J N, Barnes, B, and Stuart, A J, 1973 The remains of a late-glacial elk associated with barbed points, from High Furlong, near Blackpool, Lancashire, *Proc Prehist Soc*, **39**, 100–128

Howard-Davis, C, and Quartermaine, J, forthcoming, Survey on Anglezarke Moor and the excavation of an early Mesolithic site at Rushy Brow, *Proc Prehist Soc*

Jacobi, R M, 1978 Northern England in the 8th millenium bc: an essay, in *The early postglacial settlement of Northern Europe* (ed P Mellars), London, 243–94

Jacobi, R M, 1980 The early Holocene settlement of Wales, in *Culture and environment in prehistoric Wales* (ed A J Taylor), Brit Archaeol Rep Brit Ser **76**, Oxford,131–206

Jacobi, R M, 1987 Misanthropic miscellany: musings on British early Flandrian archaeology and other flights of fancy, in *Mesolithic Northwest Europe: recent trends* (eds P Rowley-Conwy, M Zvelebil, and H P Blankholm), Sheffield, 163–168

Jacobi, R M, Gowlett, J A J, Hedges, R E M, and Gillespie, R, 1986 Accelerator mass spectrometry dating of upper Palaelithic finds, with the Poulton elk as an example, in *Studies in the Upper Palaeolithic of Britain and Northwest Europe* (ed D Roe), Brit Archaeol Rep Int Ser, **296**, Oxford

Jacobi, R M, Tallis, J H, and Mellars, P, 1976 The southern Pennine Mesolithic and the ecological record, *Journ Archaeol Science*, **3**, 307–320

Mellars, P, 1976a Fire, ecology, animal populations and man: a study of some ecological relationships in prehistory, *Proc Prehist Soc*, **42**, 15–45

Mellars, P, 1976b Settlement patterns and industrial variability in the British Mesolithic, in *Problems in Economic and Social Archaeology*, (eds G Sieveking, I H Longworth, and K Wilson), London, 375–99

Middleton, R, 1993 Landscape archaeology in the North West and the definition of surface lithic scatter sites, *North West Wetlands Survey, Ann Rep 1993*, Lancaster, 1–8

Middleton, R, Wells, C, E, and Huckerby, E, 1995 *The wetlands of North Lancashire,* North West Wetlands Survey **3**, Lancaster Imprints **4**, Lancaster

Penney, S H, 1978 Gazetteer, *Contrebis*, **6**, 43

Poole, S, 1986 A late Mesolithic and early Bronze Age site at Piethorn Brook, Milnrow, *Greater Manchester Archaeol Journ*, **2**, 11–30

Price, T D, 1978 Mesolithic settlement systems in the Netherlands, in *The early postglacial settlement of Northern Europe*, (ed P Mellars), London, 81–114

Radley, J, and Mellars, P, 1964 A Mesolithic structure at Deepcar, Yorkshire and the affinities of its associated flint industries, *Proc Prehist Soc*, **30**, 1–24

Salisbury, C R, 1986 Comments on Kirkhead Cave, an upper Palaeolithic site in northern England, *Proc Prehist Soc*, **52**, 321–23

Salisbury, C R, 1988 Late Upper Palaeolithic artefacts from Lindale Low Cave, Cumbria, *Antiquity*, **62**, 510–513

Salisbury, C R, and Sheppard, D, 1994 The Mesolithic occupation of Heysham Head, Lancashire, *Trans Lancashire Cheshire Antiq Soc*, **87**, 141–149

Schofield, A J, 1991 Artefact distributions as activity areas: examples from South East Hampshire, in *Interpreting artefact scatters; contributions to ploughzone archaeology*, (ed A J Schofield), Oxbow Monograph **4**, Oxford, 117–128

Spencer, A, 1951 Preliminary report on archaeological investigations near Radcliffe, Manchester, *Trans Lancashire Cheshire Antiq Soc*, **42**, 196–203

Stonehouse, P, 1986 Dean Clough 1: a late Mesolithic site in the Central Pennines, *Greater Manchester Archaeol Journ*, **2**, 1–9

Stonehouse, P, 1989 Mesolithic sites on the Pennine watershed, *Greater Manchester Archaeol Journ*, **3**, 5–17

Stonehouse, P, 1994 Mesolithic sites on the Pennine watershed part II, *Archaeol North West*, **8 (2) pt II**, 38–47

Tipping, R, 1986 The stratigraphy of Kirkhead Cave, an upper Palaeolithic site in northern England: a comment, *Proc Prehist Soc*, **52**, 323–26

Tooley, M J, 1978 *Sea level changes in North West England during the Flandrian Stage*, Oxford

Williams, C T, 1985 *Mesolithic exploitation patterns in the Central Pennines, a palynological study of Soyland Moor*, British Archaeol Rep **139**, Oxford

Wymer, J J, and Bonsall, C J, 1977 *Gazetteer of Mesolithic sites in England and Wales*, CBA Res Rep **20**, London

Zvelebil, M (ed), 1986 *Hunters in transition*, Cambridge

Zvelebil, M, 1994 Plant use in the Mesolithic and its role in the transition to farming, *Proc Prehist Soc*, **60**, 35–74

3

THE NEOLITHIC AND BRONZE AGE

by Robert Middleton

This paper seeks to cover a very broad period from the earliest farming communities, with their origins in the hunter-fishers of the late Mesolithic, to the developed and established farming systems of the late Bronze Age. The area to be discussed encompasses the post-1974 county of Lancashire which excludes the Furness peninsula and the Mersey Basin. The period under discussion runs from the beginning of the early Neolithic at *c* 4000 cal BC to the end of the late Bronze Age at *c* 700 cal BC. The main divisions within this broad time span are as follows:

Early Neolithic	4000 cal BC–3200 cal BC
Late Neolithic/early Bronze Age	3200 cal BC–1650 cal BC
Late Bronze Age	1650 cal BC–700 cal BC

This dating framework has been established by radiocarbon determinations from sites across the country with shared and temporally-distinct features. Unfortunately the number of accurately dated sites in the county is small, and so any discussion of the periods must, by necessity, take a broad-brush approach. Long, well-dated palaeoecological sequences, however, are known from within the county, for example at Fenton Cottage, Winmarleigh Moss, and Thwaite House Moss (Middleton *et al* 1995) in the north and Red Moss (Hibbert *et al* 1971) and Hoscar Moss (Cundhill 1981) to the south. These have revealed the pattern of vegetation change and human impact on the environment for the whole of the period under discussion. Also of importance is the work of Tooley (*eg* 1978) on sea-level change in South West Lancashire and the Fylde.

Our view of the period in Lancashire has been shaped by only a few excavations and surveys. Key sites include the Bleasdale Circle (Dawkins 1900; Varley 1938), Kate's Pad trackway (Sobee 1953), Ben Edwards' excavation at Bonds Farm (Edwards 1991), and LUAU's work at Manor Farm (Olivier 1988). Landscape surveys have included

Anglezarke Moor (Howard-Davis and Quartermaine forthcoming) and the ongoing work of the North West Wetlands Survey in the lowland wetlands (Middleton *et al* 1995; Middleton and Browell 1994; Middleton and Tooley in prep). Summaries of prehistoric material from the county have included Sobee's (1953) collation of the Pilling Moss finds and Thornber's (1837, 1850, 1851) work in the Fylde.

Late Mesolithic / early Neolithic

The origins of the earliest farming communities lie in late Mesolithic hunter-fisher communities. Nationally, it seems that late Mesolithic people gradually adopted Neolithic traits. New technology included the use of leaf-shaped arrowheads in the place of microliths as projectile points, and the introduction of polished axes. The most important economic change was the adoption of agriculture and the management of domesticated animals.

The impetus behind these changes may have involved an increase in population at the end of the Mesolithic in favourable locations, notably on the coast, including the establishment of year-round settlements (Bonsall 1980). Recent work on the late Mesolithic in Lancashire has revealed a number of sites in coastal and riverine locations including Heysham Head (Salisbury and Sheppard 1994), Marle's Wood (Hallam pers comm), Peel (Middleton *et al* 1995), Banks (Middleton and Tooley in prep), Halton Park (Penney 1978), and Mawdesley (Hallam pers comm, Jacobi pers comm). All have been identified by surface flintwork. This is distinguished by the presence of blades removed from small cores usually made of relatively good quality flint. Implements, notably microliths and scrapers, are rare, except for those from Mawdesley (Jacobi pers comm; Wymer 1977, 168). None of these sites has been accurately dated, however, although they may belong to the latter part of the Mesolithic. Clarification of their nature and extent is urgently required if we are to understand the processes of change that led to the development of farming.

In the early Neolithic lithic scatters remain by far the most common source of evidence. The main features of the lithic assemblages continue from the preceding period. The main changes were the replacement of microliths with single piece, leaf-shaped arrowheads and the appearance of polished stone axes, usually as isolated finds. There are also some indications that the range of raw materials becomes more restricted; in particular black Pendleside chert disappears from assemblages. Scrapers remain the most common formal implement type although they vary greatly in morphology, perhaps related to their function. Leaf-shaped arrowheads are most often found as isolated finds, perhaps as casual losses from hunting and related activities. Most of the sites are dominated by flint knapping debris, including unretouched flakes. Only small numbers of cores occur.

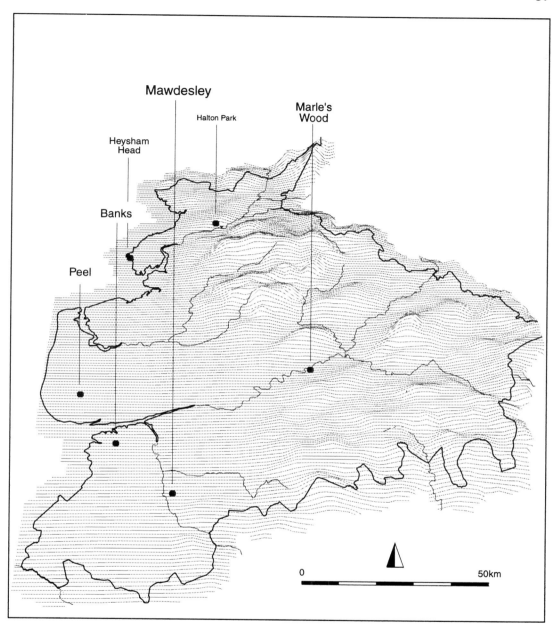

Later Mesolithic sites mentioned in the text

Complete, or near complete, axes have been found widely over the county in a variety of topographic locations. Recent work has established that these axes need not be just casual losses, but they may have had a ritual significance, either related to the axe, or to the place of deposition (Bradley and Edmonds 1993). The nature of axe procurement, exchange, and deposition changed through the Neolithic and so, unless the precise details of deposition and context are known, there are great difficulties in assessing the implications of the finds. Where thin-sectioning has been undertaken, the results suggest that most of the axes derive from Great Langdale in Cumbria (Clough and Cummins 1988, 219–221).

There is some evidence to suggest that rivers and wetlands were important places for deposition, and it is notable that the axes from Lancashire have a definite riverine and mossland distribution. It was thought that this reflected patterns of trade. It is now clear, however, that many of the axes must have been deposited deliberately and the rivers had a specific significance. Some of the mires may also have been important at this time for both settlement and the deposition of axes. For example, a group of eight axes and polishers have been found in the north and east portions of Pilling Moss which are said to have come from under the peat, and so probably have a date in the earlier part of the Neolithic. The discovery of some of the axes within the roots of standing trees may suggest some measure of deliberate deposition rather than casual loss (Middleton *et al* 1995). Similar activity is known from the uplands, such as the pair of polished axes found in peat at Delph Reservoir on the Bolton Moors (Hallam 1970, 234).

The other major new technological advance at the beginning of the Neolithic was the first use of pottery which probably augmented the earlier use of organic containers by Mesolithic communities. Pottery finds are, however, very poorly represented in Lancashire. The most reliable evidence comes from Portfield Camp, Whalley where excavations of the later hillfort revealed a truncated pit containing sherds of plain bowl pottery (Beswick and Coombs 1986). A sherd of similar material has also been found at St Michael's on the floodplain of the River Wyre in a context dating to *c* 3600–3350 cal BC (Middleton *et al* 1995, 57–59). A vessel of the Peterborough tradition has been found in Lancaster, although its context is unclear (White 1974).

Despite the apparently enormous implications of the change to farming, the gradual incorporation of Neolithic elements into existing society means that much of the economy may have remained relatively unaltered. There is an increasing body of evidence to suggest that there was substantial management and control of wild resources by Mesolithic people (Zvelebil 1994). This is most commonly shown by the extensive evidence for burning episodes from both upland and lowland situations, These may represent the clearing of scrub and light woodland to attract animals to specific locations at which they could be hunted (Jacobi *et al* 1976). There is now substantial evidence from the mires of Lancashire that such episodes were taking place from the earliest Mesolithic through to the Bronze Age. It is not clear how much of this was caused by people, although its ubiquity suggests it may represent deliberate management of the environment (Hall *et al* 1995, ch 6; Middleton *et al* 1995, ch 8).

The earliest direct evidence for a change in economic production during the Neolithic comes from pollen diagrams. Barnes (1975), for example, recorded a cereal grain associated with limited evidence for clearance and soil erosion at Rawcliffe Moss in Over Wyre. Recent work at nearby Fenton Cottage has tentatively identified cereal pollen. This may suggest that limited arable agriculture was being practised nearby (Middleton *et al* 1995, 141–152). Similar evidence has been identified from Hawes Water (Oldfield 1960) and Little Haweswater (Taylor *et al* 1994) both near Silverdale. The limited extent of the evidence, however, suggests that cereal cultivation can never have played a large part in the economy of the Neolithic. Whether this was a local or wider feature of the Neolithic is unclear, but recent research on human bones from central and southern England suggests that Neolithic peoples had a largely meat-based diet (Richards 1996).

It may be significant that cereal grains only seem to occur within a limited time span around the Elm Decline, which is dated regionally to *c* 3990–3640 cal BC (Hibbert *et al* 1971). There is little evidence for cereals either earlier, in the Mesolithic, or later, in the Neolithic and Bronze Age. It may represent an attempt, perhaps unsuccessful, to grow cereals early in the development of farming. Why cereal cultivation did not continue can only be speculated upon, although it has been suggested that the British Isles, particularly in its colder and wetter parts, was always marginal for early types of cereals (*see* Kinnes 1989). It may be significant in this context that the numbers of serrated flakes, which can be diagnostic of the early Neolithic and may be associated with cereal cultivation or processing, are very rare in Lancashire.

It is assumed that much of the economy would have depended upon the herding of animals, although the absence of Neolithic and Bronze Age faunal assemblages from the county is a problem. Evidence from other parts of the country suggests that cattle were particularly important with lesser numbers of sheep/goats and pigs. However, the use of wild resources should not be underestimated; the coastal and riverine nature of the settlement pattern may suggest that fishing continued to be important.

Fortunately, there is more evidence for the nature of settlement, although in common with most of the country, it is as tantalising as it is conclusive in the interpretation of early Neolithic occupation of the landscape. The most detailed survey which has co-ordinated palaeoecological and archaeological work to identify Neolithic settlements is that at Little Haweswater (Taylor *et al* 1994). The results suggest early Neolithic activity involved the creation of small clearances within a well-wooded environment.

Cereal cultivation early in the period appears to have been associated with settlement on the wetland edge. The disturbance of the ground cover was sufficient to create a thin deposit of hillwash within which unrolled flints have been found. Identifiable structures were absent and the main evidence for occupation was in the form of diffuse scatters of artefacts (*ibid*).

A similar pattern was revealed at nearby Storrs Moss, which was investigated by Liverpool University in the late 1960s (Powell *et al* 1971). Small trenches were excavated on the edge of what is now the Leighton Moss nature reserve, with the aim of identifying settlement traces in an area where two polished stone axes had been found. The excavation revealed a similar pattern of artefact dispersal to Little Haweswater, although it was associated with a possible wooden platform and 'postholes'. The wood was dated to 3694–3384 cal BC, although disturbance by *Phragmites* (reeds) roots made this a minimum age only; a true date on stratigraphic grounds was considered to be nearer 4333–4241 cal BC. Although these details were contained in the published report (*ibid*), the situation was confused by the discovery of a possible late Mesolithic occupation beneath the Neolithic strata to the south of the original excavations. It is thought that the finds from the Neolithic layers may have come from the earlier deposits beneath (Davey pers comm).

Neolithic features are very rare and the pits from Portfield Camp are the exception (Beswick and Coombs 1986, 173–74). Although severely truncated, the pits do have general similarities to features found in contemporary 'pit and posthole' settlements in southern and eastern England and form typical settlement evidence. Such sites are represented on the surface by diffuse scatters of worked flints.

The distribution of lithic sites suggests that settlement was concentrated in the lowlands, mainly around the coasts and in the river valleys, mirroring the late Mesolithic pattern. The relative absence of Neolithic material from the uplands, with the exception of arrowhead finds, is notable. Only scattered Neolithic material within mixed assemblages have been recovered, for example from Worsthorne Moor (Leach 1951). Early farming communities preferred well-drained soils in a county where much of the landscape is covered by heavy clays or is relatively infertile. This is shown by the evidence from Pilling Moss where there is a cluster of early Neolithic sites on the eastern edge of the moss, each located on a small patch of well-drained gravel within a poorly-drained boulder clay landscape (Middleton *et al* 1995, 56–60).

The problems of detecting occupation sites are nowhere clearer than in river valleys, where settlements themselves are likely to be covered with river-borne clays and silts. This is demonstrated by a site at St Michael's on the floodplain of the River Wyre. Flints and pottery were found in a layer of peat dating to *c* 3600–3350 cal BC containing plant remains indicative of settlement, sealed beneath 2m of alluvium (*ibid*, 57–59). Many more such sites will exist undetected beneath alluvial silts and clays on the floodplains of the county's rivers.

One of the distinctive characteristics of the Neolithic is the first use of formal burial structures in the form of long barrows and cairns. The North West, particularly Lancashire, has, however, a relative paucity of such monuments in comparison to the neighbouring Lake District (Manby 1970) or the Derbyshire Peak District (Manby 1958). In any consideration of the number of monuments in Lancashire, it must be remembered that very little survey work has been undertaken in the uplands where these monuments tend to occur. In the lowlands past agricultural activities may have led to the destruction of such monuments.

Only two long barrows are known from Lancashire, both of them located on Anglezarke Moor, a western outlier of the Pennine chain near Chorley. The most famous of these is Pikestones, located on the south-west facing slope of the moor. It has attracted interest for a number of years due to its isolation and as the only claimed

The Pikestones: a Neolithic chambered long cairn on Anglezarke Moor

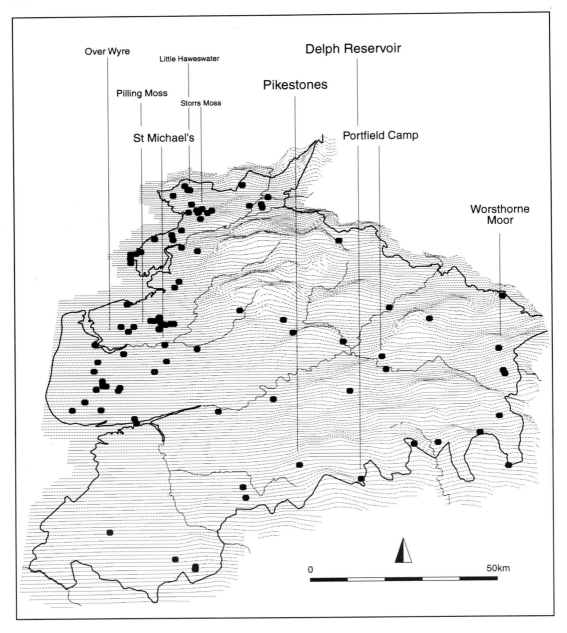

Neolithic sites in Lancashire: sites annotated above are referred to in the text

example of a Severn-Cotswold tomb north of the Cotswolds (Bu'Lock 1958). Whilst it shares a number of features in common with such tombs, including stone construction, a facade, a trapezoidal outline, and a burial chamber leading from a short passage with an opening in the middle of the facade, there must be some doubt as to whether it can be associated with morphologically similar monuments so far away (Lynch 1966). The lack of work on the monument means that many questions regarding its dating, origins, and development remain to be answered.

The survey of Anglezarke in the 1980s identified the remains of an additional tomb on the west facing slope of the same moor. Although largely ruined, it appears to comprise a small, pear-shaped cairn with a chamber formed by unworked uprights. It bears some similarity to the Neolithic cairns of Cumbria and Northumbria, although no further work has been undertaken at the site since its discovery and so all conclusions must remain tentative at this stage (Howard-Davis and Quartermaine forthcoming).

Late Neolithic / Bronze Age

In the centuries around 3200 BC there are many changes in the archaeological record across the whole of the British Isles. At this time the early farming communities seem to have developed more stable and stratified societies. There is evidence for the emergence of social elites, along with the development of a diverse range of ceremonial monuments. Henges and stone circles appear for the first time, as do individual graves under round mounds. From *c* 2200 cal BC metalwork was gradually adopted.

This period also saw changes in lithic technology with the decline of the blade-base flint knapping strategies employed in the earlier Neolithic, to be replaced by cruder, flake-based flint working associated with a new range of implement types. These include the change from leaf-shaped arrowheads to chisel and oblique forms and the first evidence for two traditions of flint working; finely-made and pressure flaked knives, scrapers, and arrowheads can be separated from everyday tools which became cruder. Changes are also apparent in the manner in which raw materials were acquired. Through the late Neolithic and into the Bronze Age, the variety and quality of raw materials declines and there is more use of very poor quality local flint.

One of the most distinctive features of the Bronze Age of Lancashire is the relatively large numbers of perforated stone objects and bronze implements that have been recovered as casual finds. The former, which are predominately axe-hammers, have a marked concentration in north Lancashire and southern Cumbria, a feature that may relate to suitable stone sources available in the area. None of the finds, however, is associated with other archaeological remains, so their mode of use and deposition is far from clear. Although dating evidence is sparse, national parallels suggest that

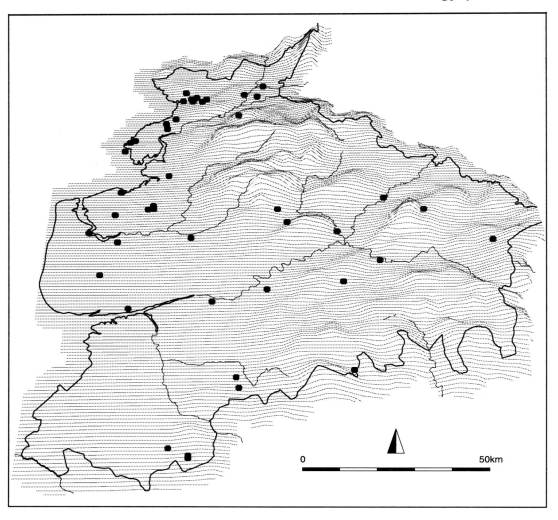

The distribution of Neolithic polished axes in Lancashire

axe-hammers and other perforated stone implements were being deposited in the earlier part of the Bronze Age, between *c* 2500–1650 cal BC. These implements tend to be found in 'dryland' locations with a generally even spread across the landscape. Clusters at Lancaster and Preston are exceptions which reflect the importance of the Rivers Lune and Ribble. That the finds cluster in lowland areas may reflect the main areas of settlement, although whether these were objects directly associated with occupation is open to question.

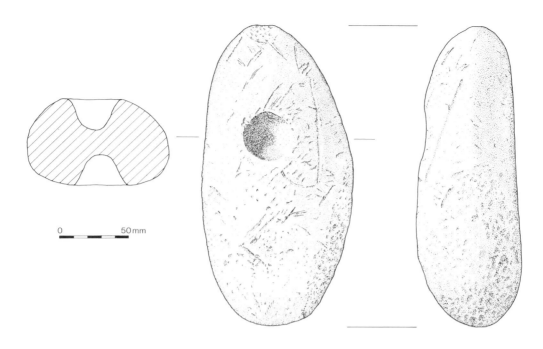

Bronze Age axe-hammer from Ridgeway Farm, Lytham Moss

It is significant that contemporary metalwork, whilst still showing a concentration in the lowlands, is markedly skewed towards the wetlands, with 75% of the finds from Lancashire deriving from wetlands, mainly rivers and mires. Pilling Moss is particularly significant in this regard. The importance of rivers for the disposal of objects noted in the Neolithic is maintained, with both the Lune and the Ribble having major concentrations. Almost all of the remaining objects are derived from the mosses, and have mainly been found within peat deposits and may have been put there deliberately as votive offerings. The precise reasoning behind this is unclear, although it is a national phenomenon with wetlands becoming more important for the disposal of objects through the Bronze Age.

The earliest metalwork finds from Lancashire are a small number of flat axes, which include the Manor Farm, Borwick, axe, dated to 1740–1640 cal BC (Olivier 1988). The axe marks on the Kate's Pad trackway suggests that metal implements may have been in use by 2345 cal BC (Middleton *et al* 1995, 60–65). An analysis of the wetland finds suggests that the large majority of them are much later than this and can be assigned to the Wallington tradition of metalworking, which includes palstaves, socketed axes, swords, dirks and rapiers, and spearheads which were deposited from *c* 1250–950 cal BC (Burgess 1968).

Most of the artefacts occur singly, although a small number of hoards are known including a group of axes found in the River Ribble in 1800 (*ibid*, fig 21), and the Winmarleigh hoard which was found in a wooden box in the late nineteenth century (Garstang 1906). As most of the material appears to have been placed in mosses when they were very wet, any associated wooden objects, including hafts, would have survived. As it is, most must have been deposited unhafted since there are records of only one axe having a haft when found; that from Lytham Moss recovered in the nineteenth century (Thornber 1837, 18).

The deposition of axes within wetlands may reflect their attractiveness for settlement in this period. Palaeoecological evidence suggests that the vegetation of the mosses was being manipulated and regulated at this time, possibly to improve the browse for herded animals, mainly by systematic burning which would have reduced the cover of heather and encouraged grass growth (Middleton *et al* 1995). It is conceivable that the widespread use of the uplands at this time could have been related to similar activity, and it may be significant that the earliest land divisions on Anglezarke Moor have tentatively been dated to the end of this period (Howard-Davis and Quartermaine forthcoming).

The small amount of faunal material from the county makes difficult any assessment of animal husbandry, although it was probably more significant within the economy than grain growing; It is clear from pollen profiles such as Fenton Cottage (Middleton *et al* 1995), that cereal cultivation was very limited. The large number of stray arrowhead finds from the Pennines may suggest that hunting was important.

Some indication of the importance of wild animals in the Bronze Age may be gleaned from the finds discovered during the construction of Preston Dock in 1885–89 (Dickson 1887, 1888). Although precise numbers are difficult to establish, a large number of bones of wild fauna were recovered associated with human skulls, a Bronze Age socketed spearhead, and a perforated shafthole axe. Two dug-out canoes were also found. None of the material has been dated, although there is a presumption that most of the finds are contemporary and of a middle Bronze Age date. There is, however, some evidence to suggest that parts of the assemblage were located in different deposits (Taylor MSS, Harris Museum, Preston). There is little doubt, however, that this is a deliberate assemblage of material deposited on the wet floodplain, possibly within an old river meander. This material is currently under further investigation (Middleton and Tooley in prep).

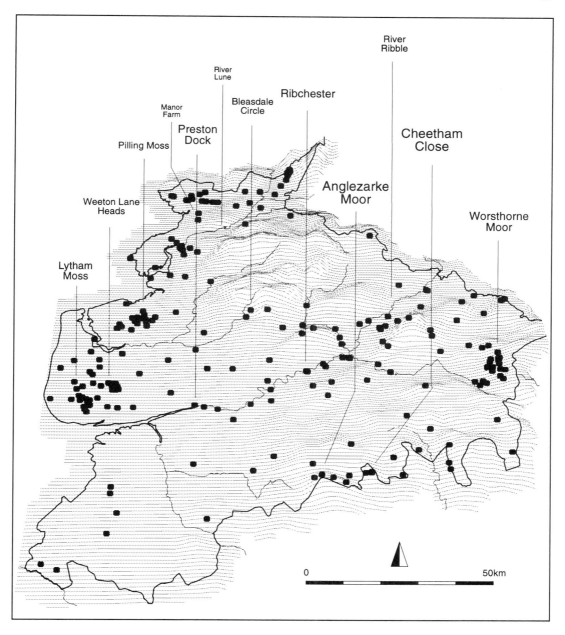

Bronze Age sites in Lancashire: sites annotated above are referred to in the text

*Stone pebble-hammer
from Greengate Farm,
Stalmine.*

Parallels for such a large deposit of diverse material are difficult to find, although smaller assemblages do occur elsewhere most of which are probably naturally-derived, such as that from Gatewarth Farm, Warrington (Shimwell pers comm). Finds of animal bones and antlers have also been recorded from wetland contexts such as Pilling Moss, Altcar Moss, Martin Mere, and from the banks of the River Wyre (Middleton *et al* 1995). There are also parallels with the deposition of human heads, such as that found in Pilling Moss in 1824 complete with 'a great abundance' of auburn hair and a necklace of jet containing a single amber bead (Edwards 1969). The necklace may date the head to the Bronze Age, although there are hints that it may have been re-deposited within the moss. There are records of two similar finds from 'peat moss' in Lancashire (Briggs and Turner 1986, 184).

It is difficult to see the deposition of detached heads within wetlands as normal practice for the disposal of the dead in the Bronze Age. There is a substantial body of evidence

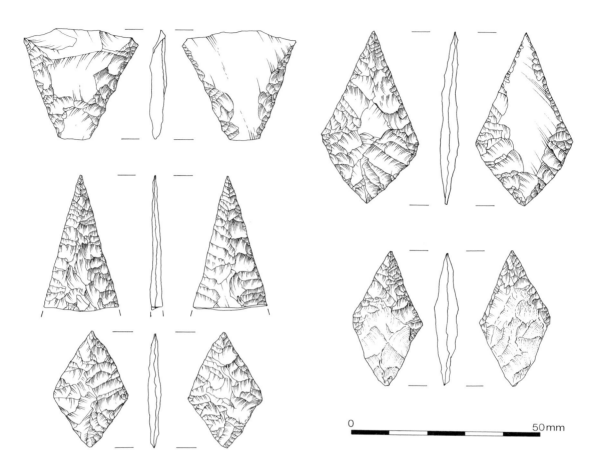

A selection of flint artefacts from a possible barrow at Peel, Lytham

for Bronze Age burial monuments, all of which can be dated to the period 2500–1600 cal BC and share features common with many similar monuments across the country. Many of these barrows and cairns are found in the uplands but they were formerly much more common, particularly in lowland areas, later farming activities having disturbed and removed a large number of them. Modern excavations and surveys have both greatly expanded the numbers known and revealed the diversity of types that were current in the early Bronze Age, as well as elucidating the complexity of individual monuments.

Relatively simple earthen barrows have been recorded at Weeton Lane Heads (Thornber 1850) and excavated at Astley Hall (Hallam pers comm). In these monuments an earthen mound surrounded by a ditch covered a central burial and sometimes satellite burials. Thornber's description of a barrow at Weeton Lane Heads suggests that some also had cairn structures within them. The huge mound of Round Loaf on Anglezarke Moor may fall into this category, although there are serious doubts whether this is an artificial mound at all (Howard-Davis and Quatermaine forthcoming).

In some cases, the monument itself may have disappeared, although finds remain to indicate their former presence. One such site has been discovered at Peel, near Lytham, where fieldwalking revealed a total of 11 arrowheads clustered in a small area in association with other fine flintwork. The high quality workmanship, along with the fact that the flint may have been imported, suggests that these artefacts may represent the last vestiges of a burial mound. Indeed, these unusual finds can be paralleled in the late Neolithic and early Bronze Age burial monuments of Yorkshire (Middleton *et al* 1995, 91–98).

Human and animal remains recovered during the construction of Preston Dock between 1885–89 (courtesy of the Harris Musem and Art Gallery, Preston)

View of the excavations at Manor Farm, Borwick (courtesy of A Olivier)

In the uplands, most of the monuments are cairns built of local stones. They range from small heaps of stones no more than 2–3m in diameter, to large examples, 10m across with built kerbs and chambers. The cairn on Winter Hill, one of the best studied in the county, falls into the latter group (Bu'Lock and Rosser 1960). It had a cairn as a core which was covered with turves and surrounded by a kerb. From the surface evidence the unexcavated cairn at Thieveley Pike appears of similar size, although it is entirely built of stone.

There can be little doubt that the larger examples are burial monuments, although the smaller ones may have had other functions. Large groups of such monuments are known from extensive areas of the North West where they have been interpreted as field clearance cairns. The fact that only isolated examples have been found may argue against this interpretation in Lancashire. Small cairns on Anglezarke and Worsthorne Moors when excavated both produced an inurned cremation burial

A primary burial at Manor Farm, Borwick, with metalwork

(Howard-Davis and Quartermaine forthcoming; Leach 1951, 19–20). Nevertheless the stone for the large burial cairn at Manor Farm may have come from field clearance (Olivier 1988), and so here as in other areas of the North West clearance and burial may have been intimately related.

The most complete picture of burial practice is given by the excavation of a complex, multi-phase monument at Manor Farm near Borwick (*ibid*). Initially, a penannnular enclosure was constructed in 1740–1640 cal BC which contained two inhumations in the centre, one of which was associated with metalwork grave goods. Later in the Bronze Age the enclosure was covered by a cairn which contained many human bone fragments and cremations. The nature of the later activity was difficult to interpret as the cairn was disturbed later in the Bronze Age, in *c* 890–790 cal BC, and in the post-Roman period. The excavation revealed not only the complexity of Bronze Age burial practice, but also the long time over which monuments retained their importance as landscape features.

This complexity and longevity is also emphasised by the Bleasdale Circle, located on the lower slopes of the Bowland Forest near Chipping. Although the phasing of this monument is unclear, it comprised at least three elements; a circular setting of posts, a barrow, and a large, palisaded enclosure (Dawkins 1900; Varley 1938). The post circle and barrow appear to respect each other whilst the enclosure may be later. The post circle has been dated to around 2200 cal BC, although the context and reliability of this date is unclear.

Excavations outside the Roman fort at Ribchester have revealed another aspect of mortuary practice, the small cremation cemetery. It was located within a heavily-disturbed semi-circular ditch dated to *c* 1600 cal BC (Olivier 1982). Other flat burial sites are known from Haulgh Hall, Bolton, and at Walmersley (Hallam 1970, 234), although these accidental discoveries may be the remains of flattened barrows and robbed cairns. Sites such as these generally have no mound and so leave no trace on the surface by which they may be discovered and many more probably remain undetected. Another aspect of mortuary practice is suggested by the use of caves.

Thieveley Pike, showing a large bronze age cairn

The scant evidence from the county includes fragments of Bronze Age pottery, possibly from a burial, from a cave at Whitewell on the Hodder (Hallam 1970, 234).

The great increase in both the variety and geographic spread of finds and monuments in the Bronze Age suggests that there was a far wider use of the landscape than in the early Neolithic. The re-use of tombs suggesting a degree of continuity throughout the period. This pattern is, to some extent, mirrored by the settlement evidence which mainly comprises scatters of lithic material. Recent fieldwalking, particularly in the Fylde, has revealed extensive spreads of flintwork across relatively large parts of the landscape, particularly on the edge of mosses and on former coastlines. This is most marked on the northern edge of Lytham Moss where Peel 'island' offered relatively well-drained soils on the wetland edge. Relatively dense spreads of flints are also known from the uplands such as on Worsthorne Moor (Leach 1951), although here the distribution is affected greatly by the degree to which covering peat survives.

In Pilling Moss a settlement on Friars' Hill may have been connected to other parts of the moss by trackways, all of which have been termed Kate's Pad. The last one found, in 1949, is now thought to be associated with a flooding episode which occurred around 2345 cal BC (Middleton *et al* 1995).

The settlement sites are represented by small, discrete scatters of flint, suggesting a relatively mobile society which would have annually re-visited favourable areas. Too little, however, is known about these sites to have any idea about the pattern of settlement or the yearly cycle. It may be relevant to suggest that monuments could have developed to act as firm markers in the landscape where settlement was not permanent. The positioning of large cairns on skylines and breaks of slope would certainly make them prominent from the lowlands. On clay soils away from the coast, much of the landscape would have supported thick, mixed woodland at this time and it appears that the level of exploitation was very limited. The small number of flint finds, combined with the pollen record of only small clearings, suggest that the mosses, coasts, and upland fringes were genuine *foci* for settlement.

The clearest idea of the nature of these settlements is given by Bonds Farm in Pilling Moss, where an artefact scatter was excavated in the late 1970s (Edwards 1991). This revealed a pattern of post- and stake-holes of little discernible form, which may reinforce the suggestion of impermanent settlement. A stake from nearby has recently been radiocarbon-dated to 1445–1397 cal BC (*ibid*) and there are hints, that the site may have been closely related to the deposition of metalwork in the nearby moss (Middleton 1993b).

It is clear that settlement activity falls off sharply after *c* 1400 cal BC and there is little metalwork present after *c*950 cal BC. The complete lack of any evidence, with the exception of a single scabbard from Pilling Moss, may be indicative of a genuine abandonment of the landscape at that time. A change in the pattern of landscape use may be indicated by the Portfield Camp evidence, where the earliest defended enclosures were constructed at the end of the Bronze Age (Beswick and Coombs 1986). The confirmation of the presence of such sites at an early date requires similar evidence to be forthcoming from other sites.

The apparent abandonment of much of the landscape in the later Bronze Age, coincides with the beginnings of the development of blanket peats in the uplands and of raised mires in lowlands, rendering much of the land unsuitable for most settlement activities. This apparent absence of activity continues into the Iron Age.

Conclusions

This paper has attempted a brief survey of the available evidence for the Neolithic and Bronze Ages. It is clear that great advances have been made in our knowledge of these periods over the past few years. Survey and excavation have revealed complex site and landscape histories. Similar strides have also been made in our appreciation of the past landscape with changes in vegetation, climate, and sea-level which are of critical importance for the interpretation of the archaeological record. Despite these advances, however, there are a large number of areas where further work is required to elucidate the nature of past human activity and to permit the development of effective and targeted management strategies.

The research agenda

Chronology: even this brief survey has indicated that any discussion of Lancashire's prehistory is hampered by the lack of a precise chronology. The number of radiocarbon dates from archaeological contexts is extremely small, and, as a result, we cannot satisfactorily relate the archaeological and palaeological records. Further effort should be expended to locate archaeological deposits with dateable organic materials.

Settlements: almost all of the evidence for settlement derives from artefact scatters which, while providing substantial evidence for activity across the landscape, have furnished few details of chronology, structure, subsistence, and function. There is a pressing need to assess some of these sites across a range of soil types and locations to establish the parameters for their management. The nature of the archaeological record indicated by surface scatters needs to be established. Do sub-surface features exist? Does organic material survive on the wetland fringes and under blanket peats? Any attempt to answer such questions should also seek to clarify the nature of surface assemblages and provide an assessment of their importance.

Palaeoecology: the palaeoecological record is proving critical in the interpretation of archaeological field evidence for the prehistoric periods. The integration of the two disciplines is essential if the full potential of the techniques used is to be realised. Sites where palaeoecological analysis can be undertaken directly in conjunction with excavation are of critical importance. Whilst such work is being undertaken in parts of the lowlands, recent research has suggested that a similar exercise in the uplands is now of the first importance (MacKay 1994).

Faunal assemblages: at present, there is lamentably little evidence to indicate the nature of animal husbandry and hunting for either the Neolithic or Bronze Age periods. It is unfortunate that parallels from outside the area must be used. If the settlement evidence suggests temporary occupation, we should seek faunal assemblages to see how animals were managed within such a system. The key here may be both to analyse existing material, such as that from Preston Dock, and to examine sites where bone is likely to survive, notably in the limestone areas near the Cumbrian border. Given the apparent significance of coasts and rivers, by implication fishing and other such activities must have been important through prehistory. It is imperative that sites where delicate fish bones survive are located and sampled. Lancashire presents very good potential for the survival of such sites given the extensive marine and alluvial deposits covering the floodplains and the coastal perimarine zone.

Future research should aim to build up a picture of the manner in which the landscape was both exploited and viewed in the past. We need to be able to provide a degree of reliable prediction for the nature of the archaeology that is likely to be encountered in any particular landscape zone. Whilst we can never foresee the completely unexpected, such as the Ribchester burials, we should recognise those the parts of the landscape where Neolithic and Bronze Age material is likely to be encountered. Thus, for example, it is becoming clear that river valleys, coasts, mosses, and the uplands are key areas for prehistoric activity. The lowland clays, on the other hand, appear to have been lightly exploited and may not reveal extensive Neolithic or Bronze Age occupation.

References

Barnes, B, 1975 *Palaeoecological studies of the late Quaternary period in the North West Lancashire lowlands*, unpubl PhD thesis, Uni Lancaster

Beswick, P, and Coombs, D G, 1986 Excavations at Portfield Hillfort, 1960, 1970, and 1972, in *Archaeology in the Pennines* (eds T G Manby and P Turnbull), Brit Archaeol Rep Brit Ser, **158**, 137–179

Bonsall, C, 1980 The coastal factor in the Mesolithic settlement of North West England, in *The Mesolithic in Europe* (ed B Gramsch), Veröffentlichungen des Museums für Ur–and Frühgeschichte Potsdam, **14/15**, 451–472

Bradley, R, and Edmonds, M, 1993 *Interpreting the axe trade*, Cambridge

Briggs, C S, and Turner, R C, 1986 A gazetteer of bog burials from Britain and Ireland, in *Lindow Man. The body in the bog* (eds I M Stead, J B Bourke, and D Brothwell), London, 181–95

Bu'Lock, J D, 1958 The Pikestones: a chambered long cairn of Neolithic type on Anglezarke Moor, Lancashire, *Trans Lancashire Cheshire Antiq Soc*, **68**, 143–145

Bu'Lock, J D, and Rosser, C E P, 1960 Winter Hill, a composite cairn of the Bronze Age, *Trans Lancashire Cheshire Antiq Soc*, **70**, 66–73

Burgess, C, 1968 *Bronze Age metalwork in Northern England*, Newcastle–upon–Tyne

Clough, T H McK, and Cummins, W A, 1988 *Stone axe studies volume 2*, C B A Res Rep, **67**, London

Cundhill, P R, 1981 The history of vegetation and land use of two peat mosses in south-west Lancashire, *The Manchester Geographer*, N ser, **2(2)**, 35–44

Dawkins, B, 1900 On the exploration of prehistoric sepulchral remains of the Bronze Age at Bleasdale by S Jackson esq, *Trans Lancashire Cheshire Antiq Soc*, **18**, 114–124

Dickson, E, 1887 Notes on the excavations at the Preston Docks, *Proc Liverpool Geol Soc*, **5(3)**, 219–56

Dickson, E, 1888 Geological notes on the Preston Dock Works and Ribble Development Scheme, *Proc Liverpool Geol Soc*, **5(4)**, 869–76

Edwards, B J N, 1969 Lancashire archaeological notes; prehistoric and Roman, *Trans Hist Soc Lancashire Cheshire*, **121**, 99–106

Edwards, B J N, 1991 Bonds Farm, *North West Wetlands Survey, Ann Rep 1991* (ed R Middleton), Lancaster, 42–43

Garstang, J, 1906 Early man, in *Victoria history of the counties of England. Lancashire vol 1* (eds W Farrer and J Brownbill), London, 211–56

Hall, D, Wells, C E, and Huckerby, E, 1995 *The wetlands of Greater Manchester*, North West Wetlands Survey, **2**, Lancaster Imprints, **3**, Lancaster

Hallam, J, 1970 The prehistory of Lancashire, *Archaeol Journ*, **77**, 232–237

Hibbert, F A, Switsur, V R, and West, R G, 1971 Radiocarbon dating of Flandrian pollen zones at Red Moss, Lancashire, *Proc Royal Soc Lond B*, **177**, 161–76

Howard-Davis, C, and Quartermaine, J, forthcoming, Survey on Anglezarke Moor and the excavation of an early Mesolithic site at Rushy Brow, *Proc Prehist Soc*

Jacobi, R M, Tallis, J H, and Mellars, P A, 1976 The southern Pennine Mesolithic and the ecological record, *Journ Archaeol Science*, **3**, 307–320

Kinnes, I A, 1989 The cattleship Potemkin: the first Neolithic in Britain, in *The archaeology of context in the Neolithic and Bronze Age* (eds J C Barrett and I A Kinnes), Sheffield, 2–8

Leach, G B, 1951 Flint implements from the Worsthorne Moors, Lancashire, *Trans Hist Soc Lancashire Cheshire*, **103**, 1–22

Lynch, F, 1966 The Pikestones, Anglezarke, Lancashire, *Proc Prehist Soc*, **32**, 347–48

Mackay, A W, 1994 *A vegetational history of the Forest of Bowland, Lancashire*, unpubl PhD thesis, Uni Manchester

Manby, T G, 1958 Chambered tombs of Derbyshire, *Derbys Archaeol Journ*, **83**, 25–39

Manby, T G, 1970 Long barrows of Northern England; structural and dating evidence, *Scot Archaeol Forum*, **2**, 1–28

Middleton, R, 1993a Landscape archaeology in the North West and the definition of surface lithic scatter sites, *North West Wetlands Survey, Ann Rep 1993* (ed R Middleton), Lancaster, 1–7

Middleton, R, 1993b Two finds of bronze from Bonds Farm, Pilling, Lancashire, *North West Wetlands Survey, Ann Rep 1993* (ed R Middleton), Lancaster, 53–56

Middleton, R, and Browell, K, 1994 Fieldwork in West Lancashire 1993/94, *North West Wetlands Survey, Ann Rep 1994* (eds R Middleton and R M Newman), Lancaster, 9–14

Middleton, R, Wells, C, and Huckerby, E, 1995 *The wetlands of North Lancashire*, North West Wetlands Survey, **3**, Lancaster Imprints, **4**, Lancaster

Middleton, R, and Tooley, M J, in prep *The wetlands of South West Lancashire*, North West Wetlands Survey, Lancaster Imprints, Lancaster

Oldfield, F, 1960 Studies in the post–Glacial history of the British vegetation: lowland Lonsdale, *New Phytologist*, **59**, 192–217

Olivier, A C H , 1982 The Ribchester *vicus* and its context — the results of recent excavations, in *Rural Settlement in the Roman North* (eds P Clack and S Haselgrove), Durham, 133–147

Olivier, A C H, 1988 The excavation of a Bronze Age funerary cairn at Manor Farm, near Borwick, North Lancashire, *Proc Prehist Soc*, **53**, 129–86

Penney, S H, 1978 Gazetteer, *Contrebis*, **6**, 43

Powell, T G E, Oldfield, F, and Corcoran, J X W P, 1971 Excavations in zone VII peat at Storrs Moss, Lancashire, England, 1965–7, *Proc Prehist Soc*, **37**, 112–37

Richards, M, 1996 'First farmers' with no taste for grain, *British Archaeol*, **12**, 6

Salisbury, C R, and Sheppard, D, 1994 The Mesolithic occupation of Heysham Head, Lancashire, *Trans Lancashire Cheshire Antiq Soc*, **87**, 141–149

Sobee, F J, 1953 *A history of Pilling*, Exeter

Taylor, J J, Jones, M D H, Innes, J B, and Oldfield, F, 1994 Little Hawes Water, in *Whither environmental archaeology?* (eds R Luff and P Rowley-Conwy), Oxbow Monograph, **38**, Oxford, 13–23

Thornber, W, 1837 *An historical and descriptive account of Blackpool and its neighbourhood*, Poulton

Thornber, W, 1850 Remarks on the Roman occupation of the Fylde District, *Trans Hist Soc Lancashire Cheshire*, **3**, 57–67

Thornber, W, 1851 An account of the Roman and British remains found north and east of the River Wyre, *Trans Hist Soc Lancashire Cheshire*, **3**, 116–26

Tooley, M J, 1978 *Sea–level changes in North-West England during the Flandrian stage*, Oxford

Varley, W J, 1938 The Bleasdale Circle, *Antiq Journ*, **18**, 154–168

White, A J, 1974 Excavations in the *vicus*, Lancaster, 1973–74, *Contrebis*, **2(2)**, 13–20

Wymer, J J (ed), 1977 *Gazetteer of Mesolithic sites in England and Wales*, C B A Res Rep, **22**, London

Zvelebil, M, 1994 Plant use in the Mesolithic and its role in the transition to farming, *Proc Prehist Soc*, **60**, 35–74

4

THE IRON AGE

by Colin Haselgrove

Our knowledge of the Iron Age in Lancashire is poorer than for almost any other part of the country and Cunliffe's map (1991, 542) of settlement types in Iron Age Britain *c* 150 BC actually depicts Lancashire as a blank. As his diagram shows, smallish rectilinear or sub-rectangular homesteads — typified by excavated examples such as Fisherwick, Staffordshire (Smith 1979), Thorpe Thewles, Cleveland (Heslop 1987), or West Brandon, Durham (Jobey 1962) — constitute the dominant settlement type in northern England as a whole from the later Bronze Age until at least the Roman period. Examples are widespead in the adjacent counties, but as soon as the Lancashire boundary is reached, the known distribution is abruptly curtailed (*eg* Challis and Harding 1975, fig 92). The same is true of other settlement types which might be assigned to the 1st millennium BC such as curvilinear enclosures and open settlements (Challis and Harding 1975, figs 93–94). While these are relatively old maps, twenty years later the situation has only improved marginally where Lancashire is concerned, whereas elsewhere the distribution of known sites has filled out greatly (*eg* Haselgrove 1982).

All told, the National Monuments Record lists only four sites excavated before 1980, which have produced features attributed to the Iron Age. Even if we add the promontory fort at Skelmore Heads near Ulverston, Cumbria, which is within the historic county, this is still easily the lowest total for any English county. Similarly, Lancashire can lay claim to only two of nearly 200 radiocarbon dates between 900 cal BC and AD 70 published from sites in northern England. In fact, both of these dates, from Castercliff hillfort near Nelson, lie within the late Bronze Age rather than the Iron Age proper. The trackway at Kate's Pad, Pilling, which was originally radiocarbon dated to the start of the 1st millennium BC, is probably of early Bronze Age construction (Huckerby *et al* 1992). As we shall see, some of the other sites which have been claimed in the past as Iron Age may just as easily date to the late Bronze Age.

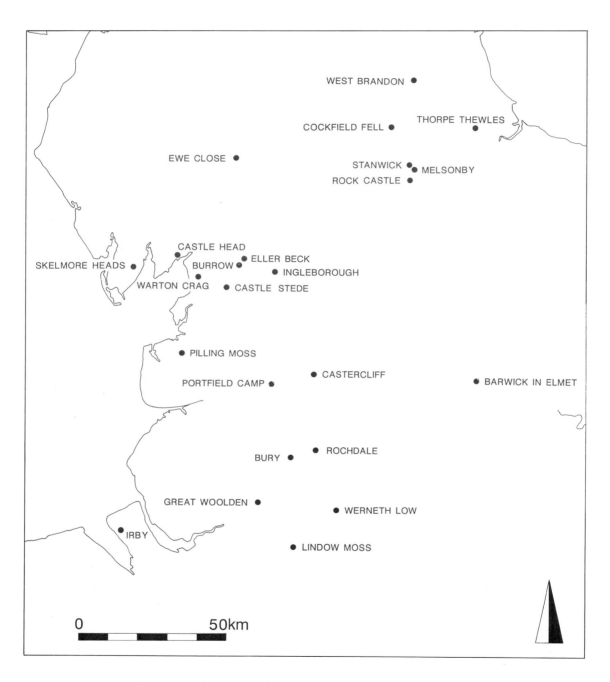

Iron Age sites in northern England referred to in the text

Economy and society

Given this paucity of material, any reconstruction of Iron Age economy and society in Lancashire must therefore start from our knowledge of the wider picture in the north of England, especially for those areas where climate and environment are likely to have exercised similar constraints on the nature of Iron Age settlement and subsistence. From this perspective, there is in fact enough evidence to suggest that the Iron Age in Lancashire developed in step with adjacent regions and that far from being an undersettled region, there was a significant and growing Iron Age population. Despite the evidence of climatic deterioration and marine transgression during the earlier 1st millennium BC, several pollen diagrams attest phases of forest clearance during the late Bronze Age, as at Chat Moss on the Greater Manchester-Cheshire border (Turner 1981), and during the Iron Age: in the Duddon and Lyth Valleys in south Cumbria (Wells 1991); at Lindow Moss, Cheshire (Stead *et al* 1986); and at Fenton Cottage, in Over Wyre (Huckerby *et al,* 1992). The massive clearance of late Iron Age or Roman date at the latter site closely parallels the situation in north-east England, where there is clear evidence of arable intensification and settlement expansion on the lowland clays beginning well before the Roman conquest (Haselgrove 1984). The effective exploitation of these more fertile soils was made possible by a combination of improved cultivation technology (especially the iron-tipped ard) and drainage methods, together with the introduction of crops like spelt wheat suited to cultivation on damper and heavier soils (Van der Veen 1992). Another important innovation associated with this process of agricultural expansion was the beehive quern, which is known from occasional finds in Lancashire (Challis and Harding 1975). At the few Iron Age sites north of the Humber where sizeable faunal assemblages have been excavated, cattle generally predominate, followed by sheep/goat and then pig (Haselgrove 1984), in contrast to southern Britain where sheep is the most frequent species. This discrepancy does not appear to be wholly due to poor survival, although the available evidence almost certainly understates the importance of sheep rearing on sites at higher altitude.

Then as now, it is probable that animal husbandry had the dominant role in Iron Age subsistence farming west of the Pennines. The excavated site at Fisherwick on the Tame gravels in Staffordshire was set in a largely pastoral landscape (Smith 1979). Much of Lancashire is over 50 m altitude and together with the Lake District suffers the highest annual rainfall of anywhere in northern England — over 100 cm of rain per annum — well above the preferred precipitation rate for barley and wheat (Higham 1987). However, we must not make the mistake of assuming that no crops were grown or indeed — as archaeologists once believed — that we are dealing with nomadic pastoralists. Almost certainly the population was largely sedentary, although there will have been some seasonal movement of herds and flocks to upland summer pastures, while crops will have been grown wherever the local conditions allowed.

Across the Pennines, Van der Veen (1994) has shown that the Iron Age inhabitants of the farmstead at Rock Castle, Gilling West, which occupies a highly exposed position beside the A66 in North Yorkshire, grew both spelt wheat and barley, while bread wheat was almost certainly introduced there before the Roman Conquest. Bread wheat is also known at Rispain Camp in Dumfries and Galloway (Haggerty and Haggerty 1983). This may even imply that it was precisely those Iron Age farming establishments which occupied the most marginal environments which were the first to experiment with the new crops. If so, Lancashire may yet come into the picture. It also remains to be seen whether North West England will yield evidence of upland cultivation comparable to the systems of cord rig which Topping (1989) has shown were widespead in the Cheviots.

In my own view, while Iron Age population densities were probably lower than in some other parts of northern England, the present lack of Iron Age material in Lancashire is probably due above all to poor archaeological visibility and survival, compounded by the notorious problems of dating and lack of artefacts common to most northern sites. Compared to Cumbria, even the relatively fertile lowlands south of Lancaster, such as the Fylde and the Ribble valley are not at all conducive to aerial survey (Higham 1980) and only a handful of sites have been found by this means, while the chances of finding Iron Age settlements in these areas by fieldwalking are almost non-existent (Bewley 1993). Similarly, while much of the county is under pasture, many of the areas where sites might particularly have been expected to survive as earthworks have in Lancashire been overtaken by urban and industrial expansion, just as in north-east England. Yet another possibility is that open sites formed a significant component of the settlement pattern. Even in optimal conditions, many of these are unlikely to yield recognisable cropmarks or surface finds. Excavations in 1994 at Melsonby, North Yorkshire, confirmed the existence of just such a site, dating to the end of the Iron Age and the early Roman period, which was found through geophysical survey (Haselgrove *et al* 1995). The ring ditch revealed by the survey could have been of any period, but was in fact the drainage ditch surrounding a circular timber building of Iron Age tradition.

Even where sites are known and have been excavated, as in the Lune Valley on the Cumbria-Lancashire boundary, severe problems of dating remain. The well-known settlement and field system at Eller Beck Site C excavated by Lowndes (1964) is generally dated to the Roman period, although none of the Roman pottery from the small-scale excavation was securely stratified. As a former Durham University student, Annabel Marriott, argued in her undergraduate dissertation, there is more than one phase of construction and the site could be interpreted as an Iron Age settlement with a subsequent phase of Roman occupation (Marriott 1991, 9). The Roman pottery could equally relate to the use of the rectilinear field system, after the abandonment of the settlement. Similarly, while some of the sites may be comparatively recent in

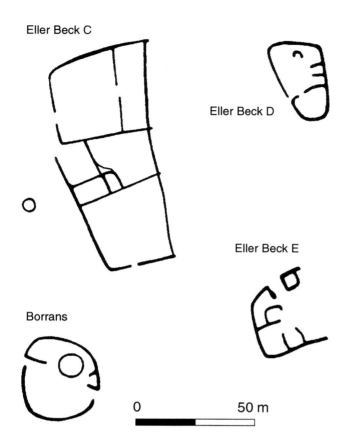

*Possible Iron Age sites in the
Lune Valley, near Kirkby
Lonsdale*

date, the density of remains at Eller Beck (Lowndes 1963) is sufficiently high to suggest that we are dealing with settlement developments over a considerable period of time. Elsewhere in the Lune Valley, the enigmatic curvilinear site on Castle Hill, Leck, has counterparts east of the Pennines, which would normally be ascribed an Iron Age date, as on Cockfield Fell, County Durham (Haselgrove 1982).

Dating problems aside, the Lune Valley sites imply that Lancashire ought eventually to produce further examples of the main types of Iron Age settlement known from elsewhere in northern England. They include rectangular, sub-rectangular and circular/oval settlements, and also unenclosed hut circles (Marriott 1991, 16–18). Very few of the Lune Valley sites (5%) are found above 300 m altitude; most (88%) are below 240 m (*ibid*, table 1). Generally, the curvilinear sites appear to be smaller and occur at higher altitude than the rectilinear sites. They also appear to play a more prominent part in the overall settlement pattern than is the case to the east of the

Aerial photograph of Castle Hill, Leck, near Kirkby Lonsdale

Pennines, where sub-rectangular enclosures predominate. By and large, the unenclosed sites occur at lower altitudes than the enclosures (*ibid*, 14–15), fuelling the suspicion that we may be completely underestimating the importance of open settlements in the lower lying areas of the county. Even where enclosed sites are plentiful, it does not follow that they formed the most important component of the settlement pattern. There is as yet no evidence for a shift toward open settlement during the late Iron Age as occurred east of the Pennines, notably at Thorpe Thewles, Cleveland (Heslop 1987), but further north, the well known site at Ewe Close, Cumbria (Collingwood 1908), could be interpreted as an Iron Age rectilinear enclosure, which subsequently expanded into an open settlement with multiple enclosures. However, until there have been extensive excavations on settlements of definite Iron Age date, we can do little more than speculate.

A number of sites in Merseyside and Greater Manchester with visible settlement remains of Romano-British date, have when investigated produced evidence of Iron Age occupation. These include Hangingbank Hill, Werneth Low, a double-ditched enclosure , which may go back to the Iron Age (Frere 1992, 280); Mill Hill Road, Irby, possibly an Iron Age open settlement (Burnham *et al* 1994, 268); Great Woolden Hall,

Salford, a promontory site enclosed by two ditches beside Chat Moss (Frere 1989, 281–2); and a second promontory fort at Bury, on the river Irwell, which produced pottery of Iron Age tradition (M Fletcher pers comm). Great Woolden Hall has yielded radiocarbon dates of 40 BC ± 25 and 25 BC ± 100 (Frere 1990, 328), while Bury has a series of four dates in the late Iron Age or early Roman period. These sites give a fair idea of the forms of Iron Age settlement which ought to be present in the lower lying parts of Lancashire as well.

Hillforts

The relative scarcity of fortified hilltop enclosures in Lancashire merely mirrors the situation elsewhere in northern England. They are generally small and encompass a variety of defensive types (Forde-Johnson 1962). None of them have been extensively excavated and those investigations which have taken place provide no real clue to the nature of the occupation in their interiors. They can be divided into a southern and a northern group. South of the Ribble, the bivallate promontory site at Portfield, Whalley, has produced evidence of an inner stone revetted box-rampart and pottery of late Bronze Age form and was probably of two phases. Castercliff has an inner, very heavily vitified timber-laced rampart — with no ditch — and an outer, incomplete timber-framed box rampart, with an accompanying rock cut ditch and a probable counterscarp bank. It is unclear whether the outer rampart pre- or postdates the inner defence (Challis and Harding 1975).

The most impressive of the northern group of hilltop fortifications is Warton Crag, near Carnforth, where three widely spaced ramparts protect two sides of a quadrilateral, the remaining two sides being formed by cliffs (Forde-Johnson 1962). The enclosed area is 6.2 ha. By contrast, the small promontory fort at Castlehead, six miles to the north-west of Warton Crag, was protected by a single north-facing rampart, revetted in front by dry-stone walling. At Skelmore Heads, near Ulverston, a palisade was succeeded by a dump rampart. The excavator, T G E Powell (1963), rejected the idea that possible post holes at the front and rear of the bank belonged to a timber-framed box-rampart. The imposing 6.5 ha plateau fortification at Ingleborough (Challis and Harding 1975), just over the county boundary in the West Riding, should be mentioned alongside this group since it potentially acted as the focus for a region which included at least part of Lancashire.

Such as it is, the evidence suggests that as on the eastern side of the Pennines most of these sites date to the earlier 1st millennium BC and were subsequently abandoned, although on analogy with southern Scottish hillforts like Eildon Hill North and Traprain Law, some of these sites conceivably retained a role as ritual or ceremonial foci during the succeeding centuries. Ingleborough is the most obvious candidate. We also need to take seriously the possibility that more Iron Age fortified sites remain

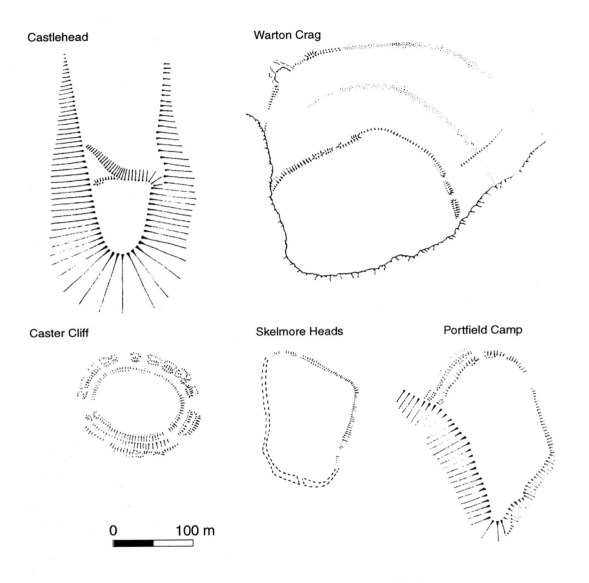

Castlehead

Warton Crag

Caster Cliff

Skelmore Heads

Portfield Camp

0   100 m

Plans of hill-forts in Lancashire (pre-1974)

to be discovered in lower-lying positions. Apart from newly recognised lowland promontory sites like Great Woolden Hall and Bury, Iron Age defended sites could easily have been subsequently built over — just as happened in the case of the large

Iron Age enclosure ditch recently excavated beneath the medieval town at Aylesbury, Buckinghamshire (Farley 1986) — or reused as Norman motte-and-bailey castles, as at Barwick-in-Elmet, Yorkshire (Ramm 1980). While the trend of modern scholarship has been to discount sites like Pennington Castle, near Ulverston; Camp Hill, Liverpool; and Castlestede, near Lancaster, as Iron Age earthworks, further work could easily make the pendulum swing back the other way. Indeed, Forde-Johnson (1962) specifically suggested that Castlestede was originally a small hillfort which had been reused to make a motte-and-bailey castle.

Metalwork

The rarity of Iron Age material culture on northern sites has often led archaeologists into supposing that they are dealing with a materially impoverished and relatively egalitarian society compared to the regions to the south, but this does not follow. In all probability, the apparent differences stem primarily from the nature of the archaeological record, compounded by differing cultural attitudes to artifact deposition and discard. In common with other areas of northern England, historical Lancashire has yielded a scatter of isolated metalwork finds, the technical accomplishment of which compares favourably with any other part of Britain (MacGregor 1976). These include a beaded torc from Mow Road, Rochdale; a bull's head escutcheon from Burrow-in-Lonsdale; a triple-headed bucket mount from the River Ribble; a sword and scabbard from Warton, which belongs to Piggott's (1950) Group IV, dating to the very end of the Iron Age; and a dagger scabbard from Pilling Moss. Several more finds come from immediately across the border in West Yorkshire, especially from caves in the Settle area.

Although Lancashire is not directly affected, a recent analytical study by David Dungworth (1994) has shown the need to be cautious in ascribing an Iron Age date to typologically similar metalwork found at Roman forts since such pieces are often manufactured from copper alloys which post-date the Conquest. Many of these items have zinc as the principal alloying agent and a majority contains some zinc (Dungworth 1994). Zinc derives ultimately from the Roman world and first reached Britain in the closing decades of the 1st century BC in the form of brass objects such as brooches and coins. Due to its bright appearance, imported brass was rapidly put to use by British smiths for the manufacture of decorative metalwork. Such objects include the swords and scabbards belonging to Piggott's Group IV, many of which have zinc as the principal alloying element. Interestingly, although the dagger scabbard from Pilling Moss is generally classified as Group IV, Dungworth's analysis showed it to be manufactured from tin bronze. Since the earlier Group III swords (which were inspired by middle La Tène models) are all made of tin bronze and are otherwise largely distinguished from Group IV on the basis of the moulding at the tip of the scabbard, Dungworth (1994) suggests that the Pilling dagger, which has an unusual moulding, may in fact be an earlier insular piece.

Bog burials

Many of these metalwork objects were found in bogs or rivers, where they undoubtedly reflect the widespread Iron Age tradition of making ritual offerings at wet places and in other natural settings. Chronologically, Lancashire follows the national pattern with a decline in the deposition of metalwork hoards and isolated finds at the start of the Iron Age, with quantites rising again at the end of the 1st millennium BC. The celebrated bog body found in 1983 at Lindow Moss, Cheshire, is another facet of the same general phenomenon (Stead *et al* 1986). There have been several potentially comparable but poorly recorded finds from within the same general region (Briggs and Turner 1986), including most notably the female head with long plaited auburn hair found in Pilling Moss, Lancashire, in 1824 (Edwards 1969). The Pilling head was wrapped in a piece of coarse woollen cloth and with it were two strings of cylindrical jet beads, with one string having a large amber bead at the centre, leading Edwards tentatively to assign it to the Bronze Age. Other finds of female heads come from Red Moss, Bolton — again with plaited hair — and from Lindow Moss itself the year before Lindow man (Lindow woman). There can be little doubt that these severed heads represent a discrete category of bog deposit, which appears to be particularly well represented in North West England (Stead *et al* 1986).

Like the metalwork offerings, the British bog burials belong to a wider northern European tradition of disposing of the dead in wet places in circumstances which suggest ritual execution or human sacrifice. While the tradition seems to span several millennia from the Neolithic to the early historic period, it was evidently at its height during the 1st millennia BC and AD. Although initially there were problems in assessing the radiocarbon dates (Stead *et al* 1986), the weight of the evidence points to Lindow Man having met his end during the 1st century AD. The careful manicuring of his fingernails would not be inconsistent with this date, since toilet sets and other items associated with personal hygiene are frequent finds in late Iron Age settlements and burials in southern England. Lindow woman is dated to the early centuries AD. Further bog finds of Iron Age date can be expected in the wetlands of Lancashire and the surrounding areas of North West England.

The end of Iron Age Lancashire

At the time of Claudius' invasion in AD 43, the inhabitants of Lancashire presumably formed part of the wider group of peoples known as the Brigantes, whom the Roman geographer Ptolemy credits with a territory stretching from sea to sea. I tend to follow Rivet and Smith in translating Brigantes as 'upland people', suggesting that this was simply a collective name given to the inhabitants of northern England by outsiders (Haselgrove 1984). According to the Roman historian Tacitus, their leader Cartimandua entered into a treaty with the Romans, which brought her considerable riches in the form of Roman gifts and subsidies, but it also led to the eventual development of an anti-Roman faction within the Brigantes headed by her consort Venutius. When Wheeler excavated the massive fortified site at Stanwick near Scotch Corner in the 1950s, he interpreted the site as the centre of Brigantian resistance to Rome (Wheeler 1954). However, the range of high quality imports found there during the 1980s excavations indicates that Stanwick is more likely to have been the capital of the pro-Roman faction of the Brigantes (Haselgrove 1990; Haselgrove *et al* 1990). Stanwick's location close to the trans-Pennine route over Stainmore was clearly one of the major factors in its development and it is entirely plausible that the late Iron Age inhabitants of Lancashire came, nominally at least, under the political control of Stanwick's rulers until the collapse of the Brigantian client kingdom in AD 69. This event brought about swift Roman military intervention — as the dendrochronological evidence from the forts at Ribchester and Carlisle shows — and by the early 70s AD the whole of the area west of the Pennines had already passed under Roman control.

The research agenda

A programme of excavation on fortified sites must be high on the agenda for future Iron Age research in Lancashire. Where the earthworks are already known to be of prehistoric date, large-scale excavations in the interior are required to establish the precise date and character of the occupation, if any, while some of the other sites could usefully be sampled to verify whether they did indeed originate in the pre-Roman period.

With regard to other settlement types, the starting point for research has to be those cropmark enclosures photographed in Lancashire which do resemble Iron Age or Romano-British settlement types elsewhere in northern England. Even if the visible remains do subsequently prove to date to the Roman period, excavation may yet produce evidence of prehistoric occupation, as has proved to be the case at a number of recently investigated sites in Merseyside and Greater Manchester.

The recovery of carbonised plant remains from Iron Age settlements anywhere in North West England will help to fill an important gap in our knowledge of developments in crop husbandry during the 1st millenium BC at a national level, as well as providing valuable material for absolute dating.

References

Bewley, R H, 1993 *Prehistoric and Romano-British settlement on the Solway Plain, Cumbria*, Oxbow Monograph, **17**, Oxford

Branigan, K, (ed), 1990 *Rome and the Brigantes*, Sheffield

Briggs, C S, and Turner, R C, 1986 A gazetteer of bog burials from Britain and Ireland, in *Lindow Man: the body in the bog* (eds I M Stead, J B Bourke, and D Brothwell) London, 181–195

Burnham, B C, Keppie, L J F, and Esmonde-Cleary, A S, 1994 Roman Britain in 1993, *Britannia*, **25**, 246–291

Challis, A, and Harding, D W, 1975 *Later prehistory from the Trent to the Tyne*, Brit Archaeol Rep Brit Ser, **20**, Oxford

Collingwood, W G, 1908 Report on an exploration of the Romano-British settlement at Ewe Close, Crosby Ravensworth, *Trans Cumberland Westmorland Antiq Archaeol Soc*, N Ser, **8**, 355–368

Cunliffe, B W, 1991 *Iron Age communities in Britain*, London

Dungworth, D, 1994 *Iron Age and Roman copper alloys from northern Britain*, unpubl PhD thesis, Uni Durham

Edwards, B J N, 1969 Lancashire archaeological notes, prehistoric and Roman, *Trans Hist Soc Lancashire Cheshire*, **121**, 99–108

Farley, M, 1986 Aylesbury, *Current Archaeology*, **101**, 187–189

Forde-Johnston, J, 1962 The hill forts of Lancashire and Cheshire, *Trans Lancashire Cheshire Antiq Soc*, **72**, 9–46

Fitts, R L, Haselgrove, C C, Lowther, P C, and Turnbull, P, 1994 An Iron Age farmstead at Rock Castle, Gilling West, North Yorkshire, *Durham Archaeol Journ*, **10**, 13–42

Frere, S S, 1989 Roman Britain in 1988, *Britannia*, **20**, 258–326

Frere, S S, 1990 Roman Britain in 1989, *Britannia*, **21**, 304–364

Frere, S S, 1992 Roman Britain in 1991, *Britannia*, **23**, 256–308

Haselgrove, C C, 1982 Indigenous settlement patterns in the Tyne-Tees lowlands, in *Rural settlement in the Roman north* (eds P A G Clack and S Haselgrove), Durham, 57–104

Haselgrove, C C, 1984 The later pre-Roman Iron Age between the Humber and the Tyne, in *Settlement and society in the Roman North* (eds P R Wilson, R F J Jones, and D M Evans), Bradford, 9–25

Haselgrove, C C, 1990 Stanwick, *Current Archaeol*, **119**, 380–385

Haselgrove, C C, Fitts, R L, and Turnbull, P, 1990 Stanwick, North Yorkshire I: recent research and previous archaeological investigations, *Archaeol Journ*, **147**, 1–15

Haselgrove, C C, Willis, S H, and Fitts, R L 1995 Excavations at Melsonby, North Yorkshire, 1994, *Uni Durham Newcastle Archaeol Rep*, **18**, 55–60

Haggerty, A, and Haggerty, G, 1983 Excavations at Rispain Camp, Whithorn, *Trans Dumfries Galloway Nat Hist Antiq Soc*, **58**, 21–51

Higham, N J, 1980 Native settlements west of the Pennines, in *Rome and the Brigantes* (ed K Branigan), Sheffield, 41–47

Higham, N J, 1987 Landscape and land use in northern England: a survey of agricultural potential *c* 500 BC–AD 500, *Landscape History*, **9**, 35–44

Huckerby, E., Wells, C, and Middleton, R, 1992 Recent palaeoecological and archaeological work in Over Wyre, Lancashire, *North West Wetlands Survey Ann Rep1992* (ed R Middleton), Lancaster, 9–18

Lowndes, R A C, 1963 'Celtic' fields, farmsteads, and burial mounds in the Lune Valley, *Trans Cumberland Westmorland Antiq Archaeol Soc,* N Ser, **63**, 77–95

Lowndes, R A C, 1964 Excavation of a Romano-British farmstead at Eller Beck, *Trans Cumberland Westmorland Antiq Archaeol Soc,* N Ser, **64**, 6–13

Marriott, A D, 1991 *Settlement in the Lune Valley*, unpubl BA dissertation, Uni Durham

MacGregor, M, 1976 *Early Celtic art in north Britain*, Leicester

Piggott, S, 1950 Swords and scabbards of the British early Iron Age, *Proc Prehist Soc,* **16**, 1–28

Ramm, H, 1980 Native settlements east of the Pennines, in *Rome and the Brigantes,* (ed K Branigan), Sheffield, 28–40

Powell, T G E, 1963 Excavations at Skelmore Heads, near Ulverston, 1957 and 1959, *Trans Cumberland Westmorland Antiq Archaeol Soc,* N Ser, **63**, 1–27

Topping, P, 1989 Early cultivation in Northumberland and the borders, *Proc Prehist Soc,* **55**, 161–179

Turner, J, 1981 The Iron Age, in *The environment in British prehistory* (eds I G Simmons and M J Tooley), London, 250–281

Van der Veen, M, 1992 *Crop husbandry regimes. An archaeobotanical study of farming in northern England, 1000 BC–AD 500*, Sheffield Archaeol Mono, **3,** Sheffield

Van der Veen, M, 1994 The plant remains, in An Iron Age farmstead at Rock Castle, Gilling West, North Yorkshire, (by R L Fitts, C C Haselgrove, P C,Lowther, and P Turnbull), *Durham Archaeol Journ,* **10**, 31–39

Wells, C, 1991 The environmental history of part of south Cumbria (High Furness, Duddon and Lyth valleys) from the early Bronze Age to historic times, *North West Wetlands Survey Ann Rep 1991* (ed R Middleton), 38–39

Wheeler, R E M, 1954 *The Stanwick fortifications*, Soc Antiq Lond Res Rep, **17**, Oxford

5

THE ROMAN PERIOD

by Kath Buxton and David Shotter
(with information supplied by Adrian Olivier)

Our understanding of the Roman period in Lancashire has been well served over the years by a succession of distinguished antiquarians, who recorded their observations and separate finds made at a wide variety of locations. In the late nineteenth century, this work was conveniently drawn together by W Thompson Watkin in his *Roman Lancashire* (1883), in which the author also contributed much material of his own. More recent assessments of the nature and chronology of the Roman occupation and its impact on the area of Lancashire have utilised the work of Watkin, and have drawn on the results of subsequent excavation and fieldwork (Edwards 1965; Jones 1970).

Despite these contributions, however, it would be a mistake to believe that as yet our understanding of the Roman period in Lancashire is comprehensive in either breadth or depth. In all probability, fewer than one hundred acres of the pre-1974 county are covered by known sites representing direct Roman occupation in the form of forts, civilian settlements, and other site types. Sampling by excavation even of these sites has covered only a very small proportion of their whole, with the result that in the cases of Wilderspool, Manchester, Wigan, Ribchester, Kirkham, Walton-le-Dale, Lancaster, and Burrow-in-Lonsdale, basic questions remain regarding the chronology of their occupation, and in some cases even concerning its nature. Nor can we as yet be sure that more major sites do not remain to be found. This paper examines our current knowledge of the Roman period in the post-1974 county of Lancashire (though references to relevant sites outside of the county are made), and concentrates on the recent discoveries at Walton-le-Dale, Ribchester, and Kirkham.

Civilian life

Aside from the military sites very few Romano-British settlements have been identified, let alone examined. Whilst sources such as the Vindolanda writing tablets offer some clues to the possible lines of enquiry, and whilst the picture of the rural landscape has yielded a little to aerial photography, and fieldwork in areas such as

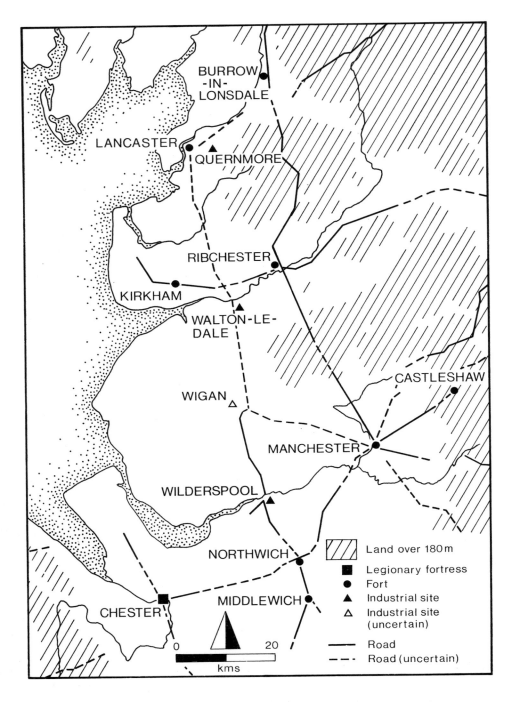

Map of pre-Hadrianic military sites in Lancashire and Cheshire

the valleys of the Ribble and the Lune (Lowndes 1963; Lowndes 1964; Shotter and White 1995), very few landscapes or individual sites have been closely studied in the area. On the positive side, however, the progress of the North West Wetlands Survey and other palaeoenvironmental investigations offer real prospects of advance. In general, perhaps, we can postulate a landscape of progressive woodland clearance in which the owners/tenants of farmsteads of various sizes provided for themselves, paid tax in kind to the authorities, and were left with sufficient for sale or barter in market-centres provided by settlements outside forts. We may also assume that an increasing impact on the landscape was made by soldiers retiring from the Roman army (Richmond 1945). Further, over the period of occupation it is likely that changing fashions and conditions, for example, climate, brought changes in the predominant products of agricultural activity. This overall view may not as yet represent a great advance, but we at least have moved away from the traditional picture of a region supporting a sparse population of recalcitrant Brigantes!

In the main our knowledge of the civilian sites outside the forts is limited to a few glimpses; at Lancaster, for example, the locations of the bath house and a possible *mansio* are known (Jones and Shotter 1988), and it seems clear that the area between Church Street and the river Lune represented the heart of the settlement. The locations of cemeteries have been pinpointed on the southern side of the settlement. Until recently, the only building at Ribchester whose location was known for certain was the bath house. Excavations in 1972 at Manchester (Deansgate) revealed a substantial area of industrial activity, suggesting that industry may have been concentrated into particular areas of the civilian settlement (Jones 1974). Inscriptions and sculptural remains at all three of these sites point to the existence of temples to a number of different deities, and the discovery in Manchester of a well known word square suggests a possible Christian presence at a relatively early date.

The occupying army would have obtained a variety of supplies from local farmers. Evidence from Lancashire, however, suggests that the provision of manufactured goods may have been on a more organised footing. It is evident that a major industrial site was established south of the Mersey at Wilderspool in the late first century AD (Hinchcliffe and Williams 1992), and a wide variety of processes have been recognised there. Similarly, industrial/storage sites have been located at Walton-le-Dale and Wigan, although little detail has as yet been established about the latter. At both Wilderspool and Walton-le-Dale, the main phases of activity appear to have come to an end by the early years of the third century, matching the evidence from the depot of Legion XX at Holt (Grimes 1930). A feature shared by these sites is their relatively short life. Clearly this poses questions concerning the reasons for this, and concerning the nature of the alternative supplies and facilities that came after them. It also seems likely that individual forts had their own industrial capacity; at Quernmore (near Lancaster), a number of kilns have been identified for the manufacture of bricks, roofing tiles, and pottery. The working life of these sites falls within the range AD 80–150, again posing the questions about subsequent arrangements (Jones and Shotter 1988).

Chronological problems

The best explored military sites of Kirkham, Ribchester, and Walton-le-Dale all share in the broader difficulties associated with assessing Roman sites in Lancashire. These include the chronological difficulties associated with conquest and occupation: it was at one time taken as axiomatic that all sites in the area were established as a result of Agricola's second campaign in AD 78. However, the implication of Tacitus' account of that campaign is that it was relatively trouble free; we may, therefore, suggest from this that politically and/or militarily the resistance that might have been centred on hillforts such as Warton Crag had already been neutralised. There is some archaeological evidence to support such an hypothesis.

The dating of structural timbers and the study of artefactual evidence such as coins, has strongly suggested that Roman intervention in Lancashire was a more lengthy process, involving more than one easy campaign. It is clear, for example, that there are strong cases to be made at Ribchester and Lancaster (as well as Carlisle) for an establishment of those sites at a date early in the 70s, presumably during the governorship of Petillius Cerialis (Shotter 1993; Buxton and Howard-Davis, forthcoming a). Further, Tacitus talks of a need for military intervention even before the governorship of Cerialis, though probably not on a permanent basis, in response to factional feuding amongst the Brigantes. Such intervention was organised possibly from Chester and would have consisted of landings in the estuaries of Lancashire of troops who would then have penetrated the area using the river valleys (Shotter 1994). Thus, in the 60s, there may have been temporary sites at Lancaster and Walton-le-Dale, and possibly also north of the Mersey near Wilderspool.

The remainder of this paper will highlight the contribution made to the knowledge of Roman Lancashire by the recent excavations at the military sites of Walton-le-Dale, Ribchester, and Kirkham.

Walton-le-Dale

For many years, Walton-le-Dale appeared on the Ordnance Survey map of Roman Britain as a 'fortlet', although there was nothing to support such a designation, and it was not until the early 1980s that excavation, under the direction of Adrian Olivier, began to reveal the true nature of the site on the south bank of the Ribble, and to provide evidence for its chronology.

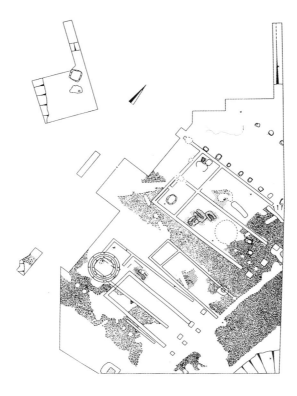

The earliest structures at Walton-le-Dale; the grey shaded areas are metalled roads

A major discovery in terms of potential significance was a substantial group of *aes* coins which are earlier than those usually found at Roman sites in Lancashire. These are copies of issues of Claudius, which appear to have circulated prominently between the mid-50s and the mid-60s, but which are very rarely found in later contexts (Sutherland 1937). Coins of this type have been found at a number of locations on the coastline and on the major river estuaries of Lancashire (Shotter 1994), and suggest that such areas represent the earliest Roman military penetration of Lancashire, perhaps during the 50s and 60s to keep the peace amongst the increasingly turbulent faction leaders of the Brigantes. This might, in its turn, suggest that contrary to the long held view, the earliest (probably temporary) military incursions were focused on the line that is represented by 'King Street', running from Littlechester *via* Middlewich, possibly Wilderspool, and Walton-le-Dale, to Lancaster. It is also likely that the earliest permanent penetration was based on these lines, and that further early Flavian military sites await discovery. Although no fort site was located during the excavations at Walton-le-Dale, the existence of one in the vicinity should not be ruled out.

The excavated furnaces/fireboxes at Walton-le-Dale

The excavations, however, recovered evidence of a site of a rather different nature, and one which appears to have flourished between the later years of the first century and the early years of the third. The size of the buildings, and the regularity of their layout leave little doubt that they are part of a complex operated by the Roman army, lying at a right angle to a north-south street, with minor streets or alleys between them. The largest buildings were around 16 metres in length, and approximately eight metres in width, and contained furnaces/fire boxes and a well. The first phase, of beam slots and post holes, was reminiscent of the buildings recovered at Corbridge (Red House), and dated to the Flavian period. The second phase had more substantial timber framed buildings probably with large doors opening onto the street.

Unfortunately, no slag or other industrial refuse was recovered to assist in the diagnosis of particular industrial processes, although the nature of the buildings themselves (sheds?) strongly suggests that they were part of an industrial complex, or possibly a storage depot. It seems likely that these buildings, therefore, relate to the infrastructure which was developed by the Roman army to support its operations in the years following conquest, and should perhaps be seen as similar to those at Holt (North Wales), which were interpreted as representing a storage/works depot for Legion XX.

Post-Roman erosion has inflicted considerable damage to the site; whilst it is clear that the north-south road was refurbished beyond Phase 2, it is not possible to say anything definite about the later phases of buildings. At the potentially similar sites of Holt and Wilderspool, activity seems to have been substantially scaled down after the early third century, although it does not appear to have ceased completely. At Walton-le-Dale there is at least the suggestion that some of the later activity on the site remained substantial in scale. Whilst many questions remain open with regard to Walton-le-Dale, it is clear that it has the potential to supply the answers to many questions regarding the support-logistics of the Roman army in north-west England. In particular, its activities need to be identified and related to what was happening at Roman fort sites in Lancashire.

Ribchester

Ribchester is one of the small number of forts in Lancashire to remain in occupation throughout the Roman period. This suggests that it was of considerable importance to the economic infrastructure, security, and governance of the area. There is no doubt as to its strategic significance; it guarded a ford on the Ribble and straddled a major cross-roads; it policed the main north-south route along the western flank of the Pennines, as well as a principal route eastwards across the Pennines to York and Aldborough. This latter road also continued west from Ribchester to Kirkham, and was presumably built solely to link the two forts. Certainly, the function of both the fort and extra-mural settlement in the first and second centuries seems to have been connected with military activity, more specifically the rapid movement of both troops and supplies around the country. Its continued importance as a transit centre for the northern frontier may account for the site's longevity.

The earliest Roman presence at Ribchester seems to have been temporary. The newly established, pre-Agricolan fort appears to have been built (*c* AD 72) on virgin territory during the period of unrest surrounding the first annexation of Brigantia. The earliest finds including such objects as the famous helmet, suggest a reasonably wealthy and showy garrison perhaps engaging in an episode of 'flag-waving' to 'impress the natives'. It is clear that this phase was very short-lived, perhaps as a result of front line troops moving on.

The fort was re-established during the Agricolan campaigns and was quickly transformed from a frontline/frontier installation to a behind-the-lines garrison. It appears to have functioned as a supply base for Agricola's campaign, a role which

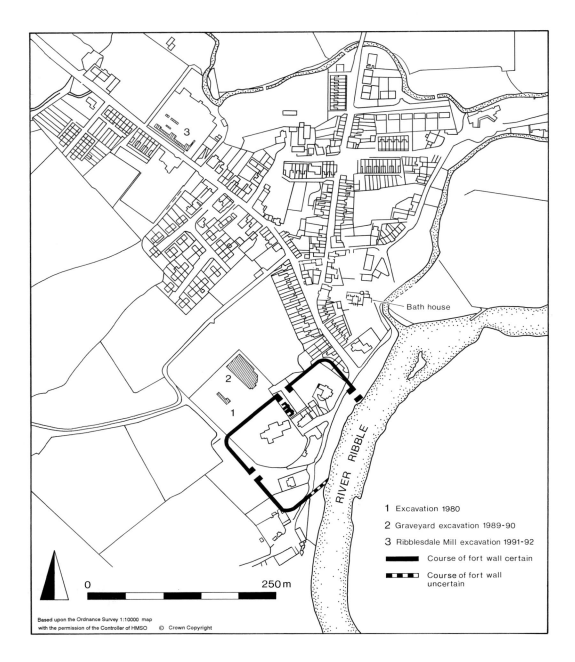

Plan of the second century stone-built fort at Ribchester

continued into the second century. The practical lifetime of a turf and timber fort, is estimated at 20 to 30 years (Wilson 1980), and at least two Flavian phases of timber building have been identified within the Ribchester fort (Edwards *et al* 1985). Presumably, by the end of the Trajanic period, the fort was becoming fairly run down, although there is no evidence to suggest that it was ever abandoned. The position of both Ribchester and Kirkham as behind-the-lines garrison/supply forts during the building of Hadrian's Wall appears to have been the stimulus for their great stone rebuilds, dated in Ribchester's case to between AD 117 and 125 (Buxton and Howard-Davis forthcoming a).

The Roman garrison in the north would have required an enormous supply network, although it has been suggested the economic burden and social effect of the Roman army may have been less pronounced than is often supposed. Once the fort became permanent, it must have had the ability to establish and foster local contacts and suppliers. There is little argument that the North West, and Lancashire in particular, represents an anomalous area within the Province, as it is within this area that the

The foundations of the industrial building found in the military controlled annexe, north of the stone fort at Ribchester

apparently conscious regime of 'Romanisation' can be seen most clearly to have failed. The reason for this failure may have been the less economically developed nature of the indigenous population. Manufacturing and supply may well have been largely superimposed on the peasant economy, the mechanisms of trade and exchange seen in southern England remaining underdeveloped during the early years of the Roman occupation.

Ribchester does not appear to have been a major industrial or manufacturing centre itself, its primary function perhaps being to distribute goods manufactured elsewhere, perhaps at Walton-le-Dale and Wilderspool. Some on-site manufacturing did take place, however, as illustrated by the leather and the copper alloy assemblages which produced leather offcuts and specialist working tools. The industrial debris from the site is an indicator that some high temperature process(es) were being carried out, although their nature remains unclear. The finds assemblages also demonstrate the presence of cavalry at Ribchester, as an unusually high amount of 'horse tack' was recovered during the excavations. Cavalry units would undoubtedly have required a steady supply of new mounts, and it is tempting to suggest that Ribchester served as a depot where drafts of new horses were assembled and trained horses redistributed as necessary. Richmond (1945) contended that the nearby Fylde was used as a horse rearing area, and Ribchester also lies close to upland areas which in the medieval period were used in part for horse rearing (Newman pers comm).

Excavations to the north of the fort (Buxton and Howard-Davis forthcoming a) indicate that there was a military-controlled annexe immediately beyond the defences, which contained large timber framed buildings or workshops, whilst, further away, there were wooden strip houses of the type often associated with civilian shops and workshops (Edwards 1981). It appears to be during the second century that Ribchester established a successful extra-mural settlement. However, in contrast to the settlements of southern England the extra-mural activity at Ribchester may not initially have been associated with the settlement of civilians and the creation of a market economy. Instead, it has been suggested that the involvement of the Roman army in the construction, ownership, and tenancy of extra-mural settlements may have been underestimated. Certainly at Ribchester a large part of this settlement was without doubt in the hands of the Roman army, whilst the civilian population (not necessarily the same as the indigenous one) was primarily in direct military employment rather than being independent traders. Furthermore, it is suggested that, other than for an inevitable scatter of 'camp followers', the entire extra-mural settlement existed only as an adjunct to the fort itself, acting as a behind-the-lines depot and supply centre for active combat and building units stationed farther north on Hadrian's Wall.

Although a large part of the extra-mural settlement appears to have been abandoned by the beginning of the third century (Buxton and Howard-Davis forthcoming a), the

Bread Peel, found during excavation at Ribchester fort

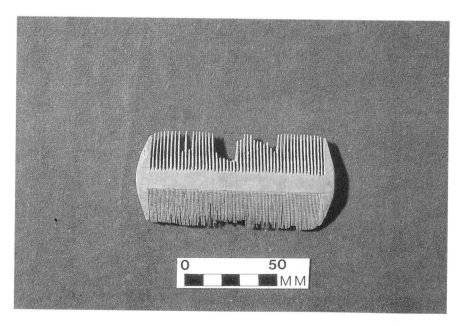

Nit comb, found during excavation at Ribchester fort

fort, rather unusually, appears to have remained occupied until the end of the Roman period. Excavation evidence (Olivier and Turner 1987; Time Team 1994) suggests the fort was defended; while epigraphic evidence implies that the garrison commander had an unusually broad remit over a wide area, and testifies to the presence at Ribchester of a *numerus equitum Sarmatarum*. This inscription, referring to Sarmatian cavalry auxiliaries, together with the Roman name for Ribchester, *Bremetennacum Veteranorum*, is thought to indicate that possibly Ribchester had become a veteran settlement for Sarmatian cavalry who presumably continued to have some military role.

Ribchester is relatively well known and documented in comparison with other Roman sites in the North-West. Even so, the site cannot be claimed to be clearly understood. Extensive unexplored deposits remain below the modern village, and questions remain about the nature and development of the Roman settlement at Ribchester particularly during the later third, fourth, and possibly even fifth centuries.

Kirkham

The existence of a Roman settlement at Kirkham has been established for many years, but in contrast to Ribchester, until recently almost nothing was known about it. The earliest Roman activity at Kirkham appears to be represented by a series of three temporary camps, defined by relatively insubstantial, successive and re-cut military ditches. It seems that none of these camps was in use for a lengthy duration, although the presence of some internal features, might suggest that some periods of occupation were long enough to warrant semi-permanent structures. The erection, on the apex of the hill, of a small ditched and defended 'fortlet' enclosing what may have been a tower, may be associated with these temporary camps.

Unlike Ribchester, finds evidence from Kirkham indicates an Agricolan date for the earliest Roman presence (Buxton and Howard-Davis forthcoming b). Environmental research and sea level studies (Middleton and Tooley in prep; Tooley 1980) have suggested that much of the Fylde may have been fairly inhospitable, lying beneath extensive raised bogs, and that the coastline might have differed substantially to that seen today. Tidal water may have reached much closer to Kirkham than at present. It is possible that the first forts or marching camps, were established to accommodate troops landed from the sea, on their way to join the main armies of Agricola's northern campaigns of AD 78. Small ships require little in the way of permanent harbour facilities and can be beached with ease, especially in sheltered water where the tidal range is relatively great. Thus the lack of evidence for a harbour below Kirkham need not prove an impediment to any link between the fort and sea access. Without this connection Kirkham appears to have had little strategic value. With it Kirkham provided a convenient sea landing, about a day's sail from the Dee and Chester, for

Plan of the second century stone-built fort at Kirkham

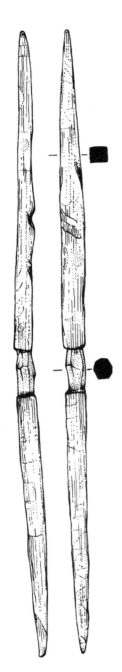

*Pilum Muralis, found in
the inner ditch surrounding
the stone fort at Kirkham*

the transhipment of goods and troops inland via the Ribble to Ribchester (Strickland pers comm). Under these circumstances a defended fortlet and signalling station, with only a small permanent garrison, would be a sensible arrangement with incoming troops accommodated in easy-to-refurbish, temporary camps. The fortlet's position close to the Ribble estuary raises the possibility that it also served as a lighthouse or beacon.

The final major phases of Roman activity at Kirkham appear to have been the building and occupation in the early second century of a large fort built of red sandstone. Recent excavations (Buxton and Howard-Davis forthcoming b) did not examine the interior of the fort but evidence suggests that quite large parts of the immediate environs outside the walls were cobbled, creating an effective *cordon sanitaire* around the fort (seen also at Ribchester). This space provided security, kept civilian activity at a distance, and could also have been used for drilling and as a marketplace. Kirkham was linked with the other forts of the Ribble valley by a road running along the north bank of the river. Contact with its neighbours would have been frequent. Indeed a comparison between second century activity at Ribchester and at Kirkham suggests that their fates were closely linked. It is possible that Kirkham (a port and transit centre), Ribchester (a supply depot), and Walton-le-Dale (a production centre) were all linked as part of the support infrastructure of the forces on the northern frontier.

The decline of military activity

During the second century the pacification and stabilisation of the northern frontier led to a reduction in military activity in the area; this must have had the effect of scaling down the support infrastructure. The evidence from Kirkham suggests the fort was abandoned in *c* AD 160. Although Walton-le-Dale appears to have continued in use after this date, activity seems to have been reduced, presumably as the industrial requirement of the army diminished. Similarly, Ribchester appears to have decreased in size and undergone a dramatic change in function from military depot to administrative centre. Its continued importance seems to have been due in part to its favourable location and perhaps its earlier military significance.

Research agenda

The sum of our knowledge about Roman Lancashire is at best patchy with large areas of enquiry offering great opportunities for further research. Far more is known about the military occupation of Lancashire than civilian life but even at the forts excavation is demonstrating considerable chronological complexity, and there remains much uncertainty regarding the occupation of military sites, particularly beyond the second century AD. Why was the major rebuild at Lancaster, referred to in an inscription, necessary? What circumstances, again at Lancaster, led to the complete rebuilding and reorientation of the fort in the fourth century, after the manner of the Saxon-Shore forts? (Jones and Shotter 1988; Shotter and White 1990). Does such work hint at the organisation at some stage in the fourth century of defences on the west coast of both Lancashire and Cumbria, and perhaps, in view of the new fort at Caer Gybi (Holyhead), farther south?

A large number of such chronological questions remain unresolved: in addition we should remember that we still lack even the most basic information about Burrow-in-Lonsdale; nor have full physical extents been recovered for any Roman fort in the county, and certainly not the information necessary for establishing complete garrison patterns. Again, the Vindolanda tablets warn us that detailed garrison arrangements might be seen to be extremely complicated, were we able to take into account such considerations as temporary secondments and illness of troops. One should also remember that the possibility exists for finding documents at other military sites besides Vindolanda, Ribchester perhaps. Though geophysical survey might provide some of the answers, for the most part only excavation will enable progress.

As we move outside the area occupied by the forts themselves, our knowledge becomes ever more patchy: the extents and organisation of civilian settlements remain in doubt; were they defended, or did they straggle into a rural suburbia? Who lived in them, and what was the source of their prosperity? Inscriptions may offer occasional clues to the identities, professions, and religious inclinations of a few individuals, whilst excavation may reveal information on activities and locations.

When we come to consider the bulk of the county, which made up the hinterlands of these sites, even less is known, and the questions which arise are major and basic. How extensive was the British population that the Romans encountered in this area? What was the nature of the physical environment, and what activities did it support?

The only information from antiquity describes it as an area of 'estuaries and woods' (Tacitus, *Agricola*, 20). How did the Roman occupiers interact with both environment and people? What arrangements were put in place with regard to the land-ownership and land-usage (Oldfield and Statham 1964/65; Jones 1980; Higham 1986)? To begin to answer these questions Romano-British rural settlements need to be identified and investigated.

References

Buxton, K M, and Howard-Davis, C, forthcoming a *Brigantia to Britannia: excavations at Ribchester 1980, 1989–90*, Lancaster Imprints

Buxton, K M, and Howard-Davis, C, forthcoming b *Excavations at Dowbridge Close, Kirkham*

Edwards, B J N, 1965, Roman Lancashire, in *Britain and Rome* (eds M G Jarrett and B Dobson), Kendal

Edwards, B J N, 1981 *Ribchester: Lancashire*, Ribchester

Edwards, B J N, Webster, P V, Jones, G D B, and Wild, J P, 1985 Excavations on the western defences and in the interior, 1970, in *Ribchester excavations: excavations within the Roman fort*, (eds B J N Edwards and P V Webster), Cardiff

Grimes, W F, 1930 Holt: the works-depot of the Twentieth Legion at Castle Lyons, *Y Cymmrodor*, **41**

Higham, N J, 1986 *The Northern Counties to AD 1000*, London

Hinchcliffe, J, and Williams, J H (eds), 1992 *Roman Warrington*, Manchester

Hird, L, forthcoming The coarse wares, in *Brigantia to Britannia: excavations at Ribchester 1980, 1989–90*, (by K M Buxton and C Howard-Davis), Lancaster Imprints

Jones, G D B, 1970 Roman Lancashire, *Archaeol Journ*, **127**, 237–245

Jones, G D B, 1974 *Roman Manchester*, Altrincham

Jones, G D B, 1980 Archaeology and coastal change in the North West, in *Archaeology and coastal change* (ed F H Thompson), Soc Antiq Occas Paper, **1**, New ser, London, 87–102

Jones, G D B, and Shotter, D C A, (eds) 1988 *Roman Lancaster*, Manchester

Lowndes, R A C, 1963 'Celtic' fields, farmsteads, and burial mounds in the Lune Valley, *Trans Cumberland Westmorland Antiq Archaeol Soc*, N Ser, **63**, 77–95

Lowndes, R A C, 1964 Excavation of a Romano-British farmstead at Eller Beck, *Trans Cumberland Westmorland Antiq Archaeol Soc*, N Ser **64**, 6–13

Middleton, R, and Tooley, M J, in prep *The wetlands of South West Lancashire*, North West Wetlands Survey, Lancaster Imprints, Lancaster

Mills, J,forthcoming The samian pottery, in *Brigantia to Britannia: excavations at Ribchester 1980, 1989-90*, (by K M Buxton and C Howard-Davis) Lancaster Imprints

Oldfield, F, and Statham, J C, 1964/65 Stratigraphy and pollen analysis on Cockerham and Pilling Mosses, North Lancashire, *Manchester Memoirs*, **107 (6)**, 1–16

Olivier, A C H, and Turner, R C, 1987 Excavations in advance of sheltered housing accommodation, Parsonage Avenue, Ribchester, 1980, in *Ribchester excavations: Excavations in the civil settlement* (eds B J N Edwards and P V Webster), Cardiff 55–81

Richmond, I A, 1945 The Sarmatae, Bremetennacum Veteranorum, and the Regio Bremetennacensis, *Journ Roman Studies*, **35**, 15–29

Shotter, D C A, 1993 Coin loss and the Roman occupation of North West England, *Brit Num Journ*, **63**, 1–19

Shotter, D C A 1994 Rome and the Brigantes: early hostilities, *Trans Cumberland Westmorland Antiq Archaeol Soc, N Ser*, **94**, 21–34

Shotter, D C A forthcoming The coin, in *Excavations at Dowbridge Close, Kirkham* (by K Buxton and C Howard-Davis)

Shotter, D C A, and White, A J, 1990 *The Roman fort and town of Lancaster*, Lancaster

Shotter, D C A, and White, A J, 1995 *The Romans in Lunesdale*, Lancaster

Sutherland, C H V, 1937 *Coinage and currency in Roman Britain*, Oxford

Tacitus, 1970 *The Agricola and the Germania* Harmondsworth

Time Team, 1994 *On the northern frontier*, London

Tooley, M, 1980 Theories of coastal change in North West England, in *Archaeology and coastal change* (ed F H Thomson), Soc Antiq Occas Paper **1**, New ser, 74–86

Watkin, W T, 1883 *Roman Lancashire*, Liverpool

Wilson, R, 1980 *Roman forts: an illustrated introduction to the garrison posts of Roman Britain*, Aylesbury

6

THE DARK AGES

by Rachel Newman

Over the last twenty years or so, the period between the end of Roman governance and the Norman Conquest has been exhaustively studied in the south of England, both from an historical and an archaeological perspective, and from this a relatively detailed picture can be gained. As a result, the title Dark Ages has come to be rather frowned upon. In the North, however, without the benefit of a corpus of documentary sources which can go some way to placing archaeological material in context, the so-called Dark Ages remain just that.

Lancashire, although it has benefited from a small number of antiquarian scholars (Baines 1870; Whitaker 1872), all of whom stand amongst the foremost in the country, has not been subject to the same attention as perhaps some other counties have. This cannot, however, be the entire reason why so little information exists for the archaeology of certain periods in the county: lack of modern research, and perhaps also a lack of diagnostic sites to be identified, must be considered.

From an historical perspective, drawn largely from sources such as the *Anglo-Saxon Chronicle* (Garmonsway 1953) and the Venerable Bede's *Ecclesiastical History of the English Speaking People* (Colgrave and Mynors 1969), the period covered by the generic title of Dark Ages can be divided into three broad phases in Lancashire, each lasting approximately two hundred years. Firstly, during the fifth and sixth centuries, following the withdrawal of the Roman military presence, it seems that a number of small British kingdoms developed. During the course of the seventh century these became subsumed within the Anglo-Saxon kingdom of Northumbria, then rapidly expanding during its golden age, although by the end of the seventh century, the Mersey seems to have been accepted as the southern boundary of the kingdom. Northumbria's decline from political pre-eminence left a power vacuum from the ninth century onwards, and from then until the Norman Conquest the whole of the North, and particularly the North West, appears to have remained politically unstable, subject to external pressures. That from the South came from the expanding English kingdoms, firstly of Mercia, but more importantly during the early tenth century from Wessex, then establishing the dominance which led to its kings becoming the

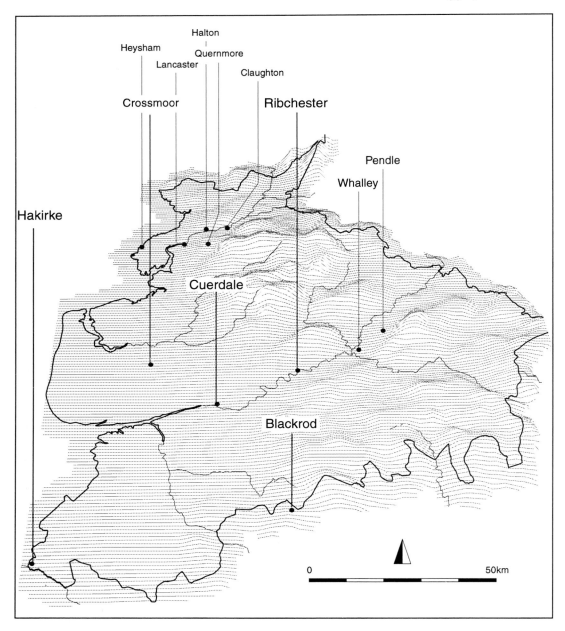

Dark Age sites in Lancashire: sites annotated above are referred to in the text

first lords of a genuinely united England. From the North, the growing power of Strathclyde penetrated far into modern Cumbria, although not obviously into Lancashire. Simultaneously, it was coalescing with the Kingdom of Scots, and this power continued to lay claim to a vast tract of northern 'England' until the thirteenth century. From the sea to the west came pressure from Scandinavian and Hiberno-Norse influences, Lancashire lying on the route between Ireland and the Isle of Man, and the Scandinavian settlements in eastern England, particularly those around York. It is perhaps little wonder that the development of shires, which can be charted during this period in the South, cannot be seen here and that 'Lancashire' is a post-Conquest creation.

The evidence for the Dark Ages in Lancashire is sparse and difficult to interpret. Besides the few documentary references, which tend to be unspecific, a student of the period has three other potential sources of data in Lancashire: place-names, stone sculpture, and what may be termed archaeological material.

Place-names

Of these, the greatest amount of data at present comes from place-names, and in large part a study of these forms the basis for most of the detailed theories of the political development of the region. This is demonstrated particularly in *The Origins of Lancashire* (Kenyon 1991), the only modern work to examine the whole county in this period. Place-names clearly are an important indicator of settlement patterns and their study can suggest clear groupings of names deriving from British and Old English words, as well as Scandinavian. As might be expected, such groupings tend to be found on better agricultural land and along river valleys; however, there are noticeable concentrations of Scandinavian names around the coast (*ibid*, 85–6). The observed distributions raise a number of questions. What do they mean in terms of an understanding of the nature of the settlement pattern, or the material culture that might be expected to be retrieved archaeologically? The survival of British names does suggest the continuance of British speech, but what does this indicate politically and when? To what extent does the number of place-names deriving from Anglo-Saxon and Scandinavian words reflect the level of new settlement, or does it merely reflect political control? In Lancashire there are a large number of hybrid place-names, with elements deriving from different languages (*op cit*, 85–7). Some make perfect sense, but others demonstrate a lack of understanding of the earlier names, such as Pendle (deriving from both the British and Old English for hill) (*op cit*, 66). How should this be interpreted in terms of what was happening during any one of the seven centuries under consideration? Such questions are vexed and the continuing debate is not limited to the north-west of the country.

It is not so very long ago that the concept of the renaming of places was accepted (despite the fact that it has long been known that one important northern religious site (Whitby in North Yorkshire) was renamed between the eighth and eleventh centuries, *Streanaeshalch* becoming Whitby (White 1993, 14); until then it was tacitly assumed that the language from which a place-name derived could be used as a chronological indicator of the developing settlement pattern. It is possible that this may be true in some localised areas, but it is likely to be the case on most occasions only in marginal land. The question of the continuance of a language should also be considered; most northern dialects are still littered with Scandinavian words, so the possibility of the continuation of British words into the seventh centuries and later should not be discounted. It should not be thought, however, that all settlements have existed since time immemorial, as many modern examples can be cited of infill development and shifting settlement, even in areas of prime agricultural land; on place-name evidence alone, one should be wary of suggesting either new settlement or the continuance of places under new names. In conclusion, although place-names must remain an important element in the consideration of settlement patterns and land usage, one must beware the too simplistic conclusions that may be drawn from them.

Documentary Sources

Documentary sources can be linked on occasions to place-names to confirm the relatively early origin of some places, but this does not give a definitive list. *Domesday Book* is our only detailed guide to land-holdings in the county, but again, Lancashire is one of the least well covered parts of the country, the information given being scanty in the extreme and, on occasions, apparently better for 1066 than for 1086. It clearly demonstrates the lack of political unity existing at that period in Lancashire; the land between the Mersey and the Ribble is listed under Cheshire, whereas that to the north forms part of the Yorkshire returns (Morgan 1978; Faull and Stinson 1986). The impression given by the returns is that the southern part of the county, being divided into hundreds, had at that period a more developed system of land holding similar to that of the south of England. In contrast most of the lands to the north seem to have been based on the old Northumbrian shire divisions and formed part of the huge estate of Earl Tosti, King Harold's brother, forfeited just a year before the Norman Conquest. To what extent these reflect genuine or simply administrative differences is a matter of debate, but it may be significant that there are obvious differences in the dialect of place-names to the north and south of the Ribble; for instance, to the south settlements around former Roman forts are -*chester* (for instance Manchester), to the north these are -*caster* (as in Lancaster) (Kenyon 1991, 139). Ribchester, lying on the Ribble, is clearly associated with the southern terminology.

It seems that the county was from a medieval viewpoint underdeveloped; there is reference to only one settlement with urban attributes: that at Penwortham on the south side of the Ribble near Preston. *Domesday Book* in Lancashire gives little ancillary information, concentrating almost entirely on taxable assets. Only occasionally does it mention a church, but does this suggest that there were very few churches in the region, or are the recorded churches the only ones included for some other reason?

Stone Sculpture

Stone sculpture is an important indicator of pre-Norman religious activity, and as such supplements the information given in *Domesday Book*, particularly when the latter simply refers to 'three churches' within an estate, as it does for the land-holding centred on Preston (Faull and Stinson 1986, 1L, 301d). The creation of such sculpture appears, however, to have depended on patronage, whether ecclesiastical or secular, and it cannot be said that every site represents a proto-parish, that every site where it is found is of equal importance, or that these were the only religious sites in the area.

Scandinavian motifs on the cross, in Halton churchyard (east face)

An evolutionary pattern can be seen in stone sculpture, which is indisputably at its richest in the north of England. Quite distinct styles demonstrate Anglo-Saxon and Scandinavian influences (Lang 1988; Bailey 1980). Whilst there is neither the wealth nor the chronological spread of material within Lancashire as may be seen in adjacent counties (particularly Cumbria), a number of important pieces exist amongst the corpus of over 100 fragments, and there is a very marked concentration of material along the Lune Valley. In particular, Heysham, Halton and Lancaster have produced fine examples of both Anglo-Saxon and Scandinavian styles, which suggest the foundation of all three sites by the eighth century and their continuance at least into the tenth century. Of these, *Domesday Book* only lists a church at Lancaster, and then only incidentally, in that one of the land-holdings is listed as *'Chercaloncastre'*, Church Lancaster (Faull and Stinson 1986, 1L, 301d). Lancaster is also unusual in that several of the surviving fragments have evidence of inscriptions on them; this is generally taken to indicate a monastic presence. The sculpture from all three sites also contains figural depictions, again a relatively unusual feature, and this also appears at Hornby.

Rare evidence for dark age buildings on the base of a cross shaft in Heysham churchyard

The other grouping of sculpture in the present-day county is from Whalley (there was another grouping in the south of the historic county along the Mersey and Irwell). This is quite distinct stylistically and is likely to be somewhat later. A piece now at Anderton, but seemingly originally from the Preston area, shows marked similarities. The most notable *lacunae* are in the low-lying west of the county, perhaps due to the relative lack of suitable stone.

Archaeological Sites

The only surviving upstanding masonry of the period is at Heysham, where elements of two churches survive, St Patrick's Chapel on the headland and St Peter's, now the parish church, a short distance to the east. This site is unique in that it is also the only such of the period in the county to be subject to modern archaeological excavation (Potter and Andrews 1994). The fabric of both church and chapel has been dated to the late eighth century; this apparent contemporaneity can be paralleled elsewhere, particularly at monastic sites, such as Jarrow.

The blocked pre-Conquest door in the west wall of St Peter's church, Heysham

It is likely that the headland site, where excavations concentrated, originated as a cemetery, the famous rock-cut graves being apparently the earliest activity, perhaps designed to contain disarticulated bone. There was evidence of a perimeter wall around the cemetery and chapel, the construction of which appeared to be contemporary with the construction of the chapel. Wall plaster was recovered from the vicinity of the chapel, some of which contained painted lettering, which would be consistent with an eighth century date (*ibid,* 120). A remarkable piece of sculpture was also recovered from the same area, which has also been ascribed an eighth century date (*op cit,* 106–9). The excavator has suggested that this may have been built into the fabric of the chapel, but it bears marked similarities to pieces that have been interpreted as the arms of massive ceremonial chairs, such as bishops' *cathedras* and abbots' seats. The evidence is therefore amassing for a monastic site at Heysham, although there is no evidence of any buildings around the chapel. The chapel was subsequently substantially refurbished and extended, the eastern extension covering the base of a cross, before the cemetery fell out of use, which on the basis of radiocarbon dates from the burials appears to have been by the twelfth century (*op cit,* 128).

The relationship between St Patrick's and St Peter's is a matter of debate, but it seems highly likely that a monastic site existed here, St Peter's perhaps forming the monastic church with St Patrick's acting as a cemetery chapel. If this can be accepted, and also a monastic function for the religious site at Lancaster, as well perhaps as at Halton, then there is clearly something very unusual happening in the lower reaches of the Lune Valley. Again, this is not without parallel in Anglo-Saxon Northumbria, but how this should be interpreted in terms of land administration is a matter that requires further research.

Other archaeological material has been derived almost entirely from casual finds, largely in the seventeenth to nineteenth centuries. This material can be divided into that deriving from burials and that deriving from hoards or casual loss. Few burials, with the exception of those around St Patrick's Chapel, have been identified, the most significant being the relatively recent find of a log coffin near Quernmore (Edwards 1973). The coffin was formed of two pieces of oak, from the same tree; unfortunately the calibration curve for radiocarbon dating in these centuries is wide and the coffin has only been dated to a period between the sixth and tenth centuries AD.

St Patrick's Chapel, Heysham

Rock-cut graves near St Patrick's Chapel, Heysham

Other possible burial sites which may be Anglo-Saxon in date are at Crossmoor, near Inskip in the Fylde, near Blackrod in the south and possibly at Ribchester (Garstang 1906, 261–2). A Scandinavian burial was recovered from a Bronze Age barrow at Claughton, which contained a pair of tortoise brooches and a brooch made from a silver gilt Carolingian baldric mount (*ibid*, 261); this latter was similar to finds from the Isle of Man.

No settlement sites have been identified, other than settlements which still exist today, and none have been excavated. The nearest site of relevance is that at Ribblehead (King 1978), just over the eastern county boundary. Here ninth century structures were identified, although there has been substantial debate about whether this farmstead has more Anglo-Saxon or Scandinavian attributes.

Coin Hoards

A potential hoard of *stycas*, ninth century Northumbrian coins, was recovered from Vicarage Fields, in Lancaster (Penney 1981, 13), indicating activity at this period around the church, which would be expected given the relatively large number of crosses here.

Lancashire contains one of the most significant coin hoards of the Scandinavian period in the whole country: that from Cuerdale, found in 1840 on the bank of the River Ribble, not far from Preston; with some 40kg of silver, it is the largest Scandinavian hoard from North West Europe. Seventy-five percent of the weight is hacksilver, including many recognisable pieces of Hiberno-Norse brooch and ring fragments; there are also between 7250 and 7500 coins, over 5000 of which come from the Scandinavian mints at York and in East Anglia, about 1000 are English, most of Alfred and Edward the Elder, about 1000 are Frankish and Italian and around 50 are Oriental. The hoard has been dated to the early part of the tenth century and interpreted as either the pay chest of a war band, or a political payment, perhaps to buy control of strategic land routes (Garstang 1906, 258–9). Another large hoard was discovered in 1611 at Hakirke, between Crosby and Formby, dating from approximately the same period (*ibid*, 259).

The chronologically latest hoard from Lancashire was found above Halton in 1815, in which were 860 silver pennies of Cnut, together with other metalwork (*ibid*). It is notable that by the eleventh century Halton was the *caput* of the major Lune Valley land-holding.

Conclusions

In summary, having looked at the various sources, what can be said about the Dark Ages in Lancashire? There is almost no evidence for the two centuries after the decay of Roman government. British place-names may suggest the survival of a British population, particularly in the Fylde and along rivers. British kingdoms covering parts of the historic county of Lancashire may have been centred on Craven and Makerfield (Higham 1993, 84–7). Logic would suggest that agricultural settlements extant in the Roman period would either continue or decline slowly; the element of the Roman infrastructure that might be expected to decline more rapidly are those settlements dependent on market forces, in other words, sites such as Lancaster and Ribchester. There is some evidence that these were in decline before the end of the Roman period; there is also evidence that the fort sites continued to see some activity although the precise nature of this remains elusive. It is perhaps ironic that Heysham was excavated as a prime site to produce evidence of sub-Roman Christian activity, but it did not. This period is perhaps the most elusive of all in the archaeological record of England as a whole, unsurprisingly since it is now accepted that the material culture would not perhaps differ markedly from the later Roman period. The major change in material culture in the North probably occurred in the seventh century.

Detail of the Hart and Hound motif on a ninth century cross in Lancaster Priory church
(courtesy of R Jellicoe)

Place-names are still the largest body of evidence for Anglo-Saxon influence in Lancashire, though supplemented by a small amount of documentary material, often not entirely helpful, such as the statement that Wilfrid's church at Ripon was given land *iuxta Rippel* (Tait 1908, 2–3). Does this perhaps indicate land around Ribchester, the dedication of that church being to St Wilfrid? It has also been suggested that Ripon was granted a major estate in the Fylde.

The place-name evidence is also supplemented from the eighth century onwards by the presence of stone sculpture, indicating religious centres, probably of some prestige. It is frequently stated that the presence of Anglo-Saxon stone sculpture indicates the site of a monastery (Bailey 1980, 81–3). Other evidence may support this at Heysham and Lancaster, but what of other sites? Very little purely archaeological information has been gathered to date; to what extent is this because it is not being recognised?

Most evidence relates to the so-called Scandinavian influence in the later pre-Conquest period. Here, we have place-name evidence, documentary sources including, at the end of the period, *Domesday Book*, stone sculpture, some evidence from the one site excavated in modern times, and some material derived largely from the antiquarian past. Together these suggest a growing administrative infrastructure, but also political instability, particularly in the north of the county. They also demonstrate centres of wealth and prestige, albeit linked to religious activity. The lack of diagnostically Scandinavian burials, apart from at Claughton, would suggest that Christianity had taken hold, even amongst new settlers.

That there were new settlers is not in doubt, but the theory of mass settlement in the Anglo-Saxon period and to a lesser extent by Scandinavians, is increasingly being disputed. It is now becoming accepted that in both cases the political take-over was inspired more by the need for a reservoir of lordships for the dispensation of patronage, and the control of key routes, than by land hunger.

The picture is however still fragmented throughout the Dark Ages, and coherent theories can only be drawn up with much speculation. So, what direction should research be taking? The answer is not unique to Lancashire. For the early period there is still a need to recognise sites; it is now 21 years since *Archaeology in the North* (Clack and Gosling 1976) cried out in despair 'there can't have been nobody there!' Since that time, sites have slowly begun to be recognised on the eastern side of the Pennines, and recently signs in Cumbria have indicated that sites are there, however if you are lucky enough to find them. Teasing the insubstantial remains from the soil is a difficult process. Perhaps we would do well to take lessons from our Welsh colleagues who have tackled the same problems.

The Research Agenda

The most basic research questions still need to be posed for this period. Areas to be targeted with detailed fieldwork should be defined: the Lune valley is one obvious example. However, we should beware of the idea that we merely have to look to find. The North West Wetlands Survey has spent several years in detailed field survey of the lowlands of Lancashire (Middleton *et al* 1995), and have found very little that could be associated with this period, although the associated palaeoecological work is suggesting that the traditional picture of decay following the Romans until the medieval upsurge of population is far too simplistic and that many responses were at a very local level. In addition, excavations of prime sites such as Lancaster and Ribchester have signally failed to find any concrete traces of the period between Roman and medieval occupation, although the single piece of pre-Conquest pottery, from the market site in Lancaster (C Howard-Davis pers comm), may herald a change of fortune.

An early medieval landscape is out there, and sense can be teased from the scattered evidence, but it is not an easy task. This is a period where research is desperately needed and we should look forward to an ongoing debate about how it can be achieved.

References

Bailey, R N, 1980, *Viking Age sculpture*, London

Baines, E, 1870 *The history of the County Palatine and Duchy of Lancaster*, v1–4, London

Clack, P A G, and Gosling, P F, 1976 *Archaeology in the North*, Newcastle

Colgrave, B, and Mynors, R A B, (eds), 1969 *Bede's Ecclesiastical History of the English People*, Oxford

Edwards, B J N 1973, A canoe burial near Lancaster, *Antiquity*, **47**, 298–301

Faull, M L, and Stinson, M, (eds), 1986 Yorkshire, in *Domesday Book* (ed J Morris), **30**, Chichester

Garmonsway, G N (trans), 1953 *The Anglo-Saxon Chronicle*, London

Garstang, J, 1906 Anglo-Saxon remains, in *The Victoria History of the County of Lancaster* (eds W Farrer and J Brownbill), **1**, London, 257–68

Higham, N J, 1993 *The Kingdom of Northumbria AD 350–1100*, Stroud

Kenyon, D, 1991 *The origins of Lancashire*, Manchester

King, A, 1978 Gauber high pasture, Ribblehead: an interim report, in *Viking Age York and the North* (ed RE Hall), CBA Res Rep, **27**, London, 21–25

Lang, J T, 1988, *Anglo-Saxon sculpture*, Princes Risborough

Middleton, R, Wells, C E, and Huckerby, E, 1995, *The wetlands of North Lancashire*, North West Wetlands Survey, **3**, Lancaster Imprints, **4**, Lancaster

Morgan, P, (ed), 1978 Cheshire, in *Domesday Book* (ed J Morris), **26**, Chichester

Penney, S H, 1981 *Lancaster: evolution of its townscape*, Centre North West Regional Studies Occas Paper, **9**, Lancaster

Potter, T W, and Andrews, R D, 1994 Excavation and survey at St Patrick's Chapel and St Peter's Church, Heysham, Lancashire, 1977-8, *Antiq J*, **74**, 55–134

Tait, J, 1908 Ecclesiastical history to the Reformation, in *The Victoria History of the County of Lancaster* (eds W Farrer and J Brownbill), **2**, London, 1–39

Whitaker, T D, 1872 *An history of the original parish of Whalley and the Honor of Clitheroe*, 4th ed, v **1**, **2**, London

White, A, 1993, *A History of Whitby*, Chichester

7

MEDIEVAL RURAL SETTLEMENT

by Richard Newman

Despite the recent efforts of researchers, in particular historical geographers such as Mary Atkin, Mary Higham, and Angus Winchester, medieval settlement study in Lancashire remains in its infancy. Far less work has been done here than in many areas of England and Wales. This was highlighted in 1989 with the publication of a set of studies dedicated to Maurice Beresford and John Hurst, two of the foremost pioneers in medieval settlement studies, for (with the exception of the Welsh Marches) these studies touched upon virtually every county in England except Lancashire (Aston *et al* 1989). The entire area of North West England between the River Mersey and the River Kent failed to merit one mention. In 1988 Grenville Astill counted 35 sites in England where medieval settlement remains survived sufficiently well to allow a reconstruction of their buildings; not one example came from historic Lancashire, Westmorland, or the West Riding of Yorkshire (Astill 1990, 40). Thus there remains plenty of scope for original research and the investigation of the many themes current in medieval settlement studies. Themes such as settlement origins, pattern, morphology, and topology, as well as the related topics of inter-site relationships, estate origins, and development, and the nature and evolution of building types.

The study of medieval settlement in Lancashire is hampered by a lack of associated modern scholarship. Whilst a great deal of historical research was undertaken into medieval Lancashire in the nineteenth and early twentieth centuries, comparatively little has happened since the Second World War. As one of the first counties to complete its Victoria County History series, Lancashire lacks a modern investigation of its parishes. Recently, historians and historical geographers have concentrated their efforts in neighbouring counties. Morphological analysis of settlements, as attempted by Brian Roberts in North East England and more recently in Cumbria (Roberts 1987, 1990), is generally lacking in Lancashire. In comparison to Cheshire and Cumbria, very little archaeological work has been carried out on medieval settlements. Recent excavations within historic Lancashire, such as that at Fazakerley a shrunken hamlet of Walton in modern Merseyside, have been undertaken in less than ideal conditions; thus the results have been difficult to interpret and limited in their potential (LUAU

1995). Lancashire's medieval settlement archaeology suffers from difficulties in relative dating. The most common artefact type used for dating is pottery and this does not have a well established chronology. No pre-thirteenth century production site has been found in the North West. Moreover, as Maureen Mellor has recently noted, whilst the development of medieval ceramic production and distribution has been elucidated for Cheshire and Merseyside, they are still 'little understood' for Lancashire and Cumbria (Mellor 1994, 47). In short, the archaeological database is deficient.

Site types

The Sites and Monuments Record for Lancashire contains entries for 42 deserted or shrunken medieval settlements, of which one, Stock near Barnoldswick, is a scheduled monument. It also refers to 45 medieval or likely medieval moated sites and has entries for 10 other sites which might be medieval moated sites. Twelve of these moated sites are scheduled monuments. In addition there are 12 tower houses entered onto the SMR, some of these sites being associated with moats or shrunken and deserted settlements. Three of them are scheduled monuments. There are few upland sites listed, nor any deserted or presently occupied farmsteads not associated with moats, halls, or tower houses. The record is biased toward larger nucleated settlement remains and the more visually impressive sites. Past conservation policies have been similarly skewed, risking the continuation of the noted bias into the future through the preferential survival of the better protected sites.

The county

Lancashire for the remainder of this brief resumé is broadly the present-day county as covered by the SMR. Ignoring the primarily upland slab of the West Riding, now included in the county, it is comprised for the most part of the ancient hundreds of Leyland, Blackburn, Amounderness, and Lonsdale. Along with Lancashire beyond the Sands (now in Cumbria), this area experienced a different early medieval history to those parts of Lancashire to the south, the later medieval hundreds of West Derby and Salford. Following the collapse of Northumbrian power the northern hundreds of Lancashire came under Viking political control throughout much of the ninth and earlier tenth centuries, whilst the southern part remained largely under Anglo-Saxon control as an appendage of the Mercian province of Cheshire. This situation is recognised in *Domesday Book* where the south appears under Cheshire and the north under Yorkshire (Kenyon 1991, 113). It is precisely in the ninth and tenth centuries that elsewhere in the country an intensification of lordship and manorialisation is seen as encouraging settlement nucleation; a process that was most marked in the Anglo-Danish Midlands (Austin 1989a, 241). Thus a divergence in the historical development of north and south Lancashire at a key moment in the history of settlement pattern evolution, might be expected to have left its mark on the landscape.

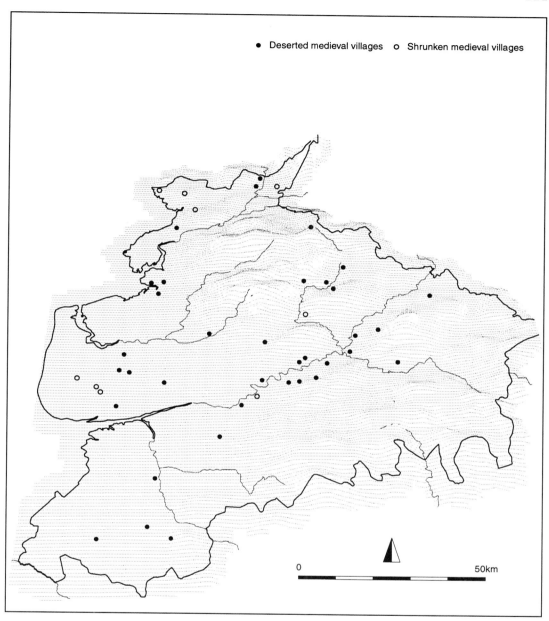

The distribution of Deserted Medieval Settlements (DMVs)

The distinction between north and south of the Ribble is continued into the twelfth century with the north being a frontier zone; indeed the Lune may have been the *de facto* border between Scottish and English control in the late eleventh century, as indicated by the mottes aligned along it (Higham 1991, 85). Scottish control was extended to the Ribble between 1139–1157 AD, and it was only after the reassertion of Angevin power that Lancashire north of the Ribble became fully integrated with the area to the south (Bagley 1982, 32).

Regionality

W G Hoskins many years ago recognised the great local variability present in the English landscape (Hoskins 1955). Topography and geomorphology can change rapidly within very short distances. Angus Winchester in his recent essay on the Lancashire landscape refers to the way in which localities were viewed by contemporaries as separate countries with distinct natures (Winchester 1993, 7–8). This perception is revealed clearly in some of the county Board of Agriculture returns collected at the end of the eighteenth century. The concept of the country, or as it is known in France and is used by some historians here the *pays*, is crucial to the understanding of local variation in settlement pattern and type. *Pays* such as Amounderness or Blackburnshire might differ in land use, economy, social structure as well as in accent, dialect, and local traditions and customs. In the Middle Ages localism was also encouraged by poor communications often exacerbated by natural constraints. Furness, an entire *pay*, was confined by mountains, sea, and the quicksands of Morecambe Bay. As late as the mid-seventeeth century the winter floods prevented travel from Rufford to the parish church at Croston (Fishwick 1879, 110), and avoidance of the mosslands added considerably to Celia Fiennes' journey from Wigan to Preston (Walker 1939, 5).

Despite the tendency towards 'parochialism' and isolation in a largely illiterate society, lacking good communications and subject to the frequent depredations of local natural disasters, there were many links between communities throughout Lancashire. It is likely that, as elsewhere in England, lowland settlements were instrumental in settling the uplands, with dependant upland farms and hamlets occurring at considerable distances from their lowland focus. The place-name Ortner in Over Wyresdale is derived from Overton-*erg*, that is the cattle farm belonging to Overton, a lowland settlement near the mouth of the River Lune (Winchester 1993, 23). The medieval ecclesiastical parishes of Lancashire also exhibit evidence of lowland/upland linkages. Croston parish was composed of 11 townships one of which was the detached upland township of Chorley, similarly Penwortham parish included amongst its six townships the detached upland township of Brindle (Atkin 1985, 173).

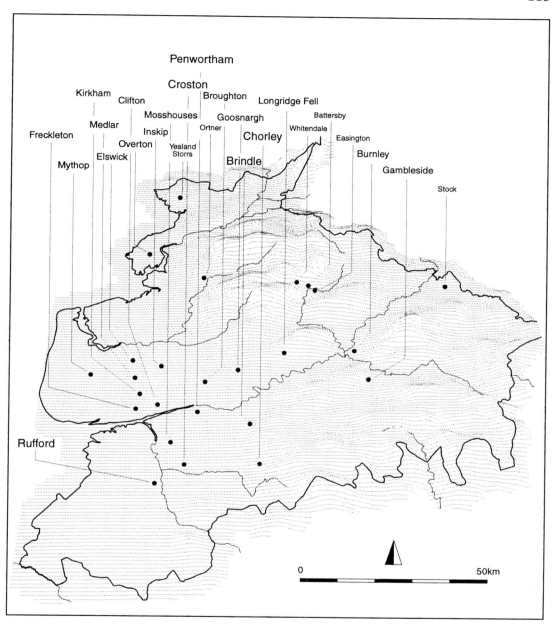

Medieval rural settlement; sites mentioned in the text

Any observer of the Lancashire landscape or reader of a map can see that it is composed of markedly distinct topographical zones. Angus Winchester has divided the county broadly into three on the basis of its physical geography. A coastal lowland zone, an upland zone, and an area between the two extremes characterised by well-wooded rising ground (Winchester 1993). The *pays* broadly relate to these zones, Amounderness was largely lowland, Cartmel was wooded undulating country, and the area known as Blackburnshire in the early Middle Ages, and which later came to form much of the honour of Clitheroe, was largely upland (*ibid*, 22). Each zone has a distinctive settlement pattern and related field pattern. Winchester contends that the lowland zone was characterised by nucleated settlements surrounded by open common fields. The frontier zone between the lowland and upland is seen as characterised by hamlets and individual farmsteads set amongst small enclosed fields, though there was undoubtedly some common open field as well, while the upland zone consisted of expanses of open moorland let to rough grazing and farmed by cattle ranches known as vaccaries. These belonged to the great feudal lordships of medieval Lancashire, the earldom of Lancaster and the honour of Clitheroe.

Nucleation and dispersion

There is little evidence for the nature and morphology of Lancashire's rural settlements before the thirteenth century. It seems likely that following on from an Iron Age/Romano-British tradition most pre-ninth century rural settlement was dispersed, consisting of single family holdings, scattered throughout large estates that may have been the forerunners of the ecclesiastical parishes or even the shires of Lancashire. These single farmsteads would nevertheless have been clustered into areas of better land particularly in the lowland zone, where the extensive mires would have focused settlement onto the drier ridges and hillocks, areas of favoured settlement location from prehistoric times. It is possible that no change was wrought in settlement type or pattern by the Anglian take over of the region, but whatever the degree of settlement continuity the names of the settlements today are, as they were in 1086 in *Domesday Book*, predominantly Anglian. By the later eleventh century the process of manorialisation may have led to the development of nucleated settlements (Taylor 1983).

In the Fylde some of these nucleated settlements such as Elswick and Clifton have regular planned layouts, like those noted by Brian Roberts in Durham, Yorkshire, and Cumbria. It has been suggested that these settlements were laid out after the Norman Conquest as a result of manors being laid waste in the harrying of the north (Roberts 1972, Roberts 1987). In Lancashire a similar explanation has been proposed for the origin of the Fylde's planned nucleations, for in *Domesday Book* out of 60 townships within a large estate centered on Preston only 16 were said to have any inhabitants. Clearly the Fylde had been depopulated before 1086, perhaps as a result of Malcolm III's invasion of 1061 (Winchester 1993, 13), or because of the deliberate wasting of the region by the Normans either to quell resistance or to discourage invasion from the sea (Higham 1991, 86). It must be noted, however, that there is no historical evidence to link settlement planning in the North directly to any historical event such as the 'harrying of the North'. Supposed planned settlements may have evolved at any time from the ninth century onwards (Austin 1989b, 145).

By the thirteenth century Amounderness and the coastal and lower lying parts of Leyland and Lonsdale hundreds were dominated by nucleated settlements. These were surrounded by open common fields divided into strips, though probably organised on some form of infield/outfield basis rather than as two, three, or four field rotated cropping systems, as was common in the Midland counties and the Vale of York (Winchester 1993, 14).

Moated sites occurred throughout the lowland and upland/lowland interface. They cannot be regarded as indicative of a dispersed settlement pattern since they are not

Aerial photograph of Camp House moated site, near Hornby

primarily associated with isolated farmsteads, but are a social phenomena associated with higher status sites. Such sites, usually manor houses, granges, or major freehold farms are often part of an essentially nucleated settlement pattern as is the case with Camp House moated site in the Lune Valley.

In the interface between the lowland and upland a mixed pattern of settlement appears to have evolved during the Middle Ages, reflected in the present-day landscape by a scattering of small villages, hamlets, and individual farmsteads surrounded by smallish irregular fields. This zone is seen by Angus Winchester as having most of Lancashire's woodland resources. Certainly there is a concentration of *leah* place-names within it indicative of Anglo-Saxon woodland clearance. Later clearance is also suggested by names such as 'riddings' and 'stubbings' (*ibid*, 19). It is possible that this zone was being exploited in the early medieval period from settlement *foci* in the lowland and later medieval estate linkages such as those between Croston and Chorley or Kirkham and Goosnargh may reflect this (*ibid*, 18).

The lowland townships in the early medieval period may have exploited the interface zone as grazing land. Within this zone Mary Atkin noted small settlements which had fields collected into two distinct roughly oval enclosures. One oval, the larger, appeared to be given over to pasture farming and was associated with a single farm while the smaller oval appeared to be arable, showed signs of strip divisions, and was associated with a number of farms sometimes grouped together in a hamlet. Atkin interpreted this pattern as resulting from vaccary farming, with the single farm and pasture being the focus of the vaccary and the group of farms and the arable land provisioning the vaccary. Some of these sites are associated with Tunstall or Tunstead place-names that may be indicative of vaccaries (Atkin 1985, 171–5). This hypothesis is of interest, but it must be remembered that much of the evidence is derived from nineteenth century maps and may not be reliable.

By the thirteenth century small nucleations with surrounding open common field systems had evolved in this zone (Winchester 1993, 21). It is likely that in most cases such systems were not as regular as those in the lowland zone and were probably subject to earlier abandonment and enclosure.

Unlike the lowland/upland interface, much of the uplands has little evidence for woodland in the medieval period. There are few woodland place-names associated with Bowland, though this absence may be a sign of the absence of settlements to which to apply the names as much as a signifier of the absence of woodland. In contrast, names relating to medieval woodland clearance are common in Rossendale. Nevertheless, it seems likely that most of the uplands had been largely denuded of tree cover from at least the later Neolithic/early Bronze Age period. Their designation as Forests after the Norman Conquest of course does not imply that these high land areas were wooded, but merely indicates that they were areas of land over which the rights of the chase were maintained. The uplands, after the Norman Conquest, were kept as demesne lands with much of the land being used for cattle ranching. These vaccaries were based around a farmstead, usually located in a valley bottom, such as Whitendale in Bowland. Most vaccaries would have had some arable land or dependant arable farms to sustain the vaccary work force (Atkin 1985, 177).

Gradually, during the fifteenth and sixteenth centuries, the lords' interest in the direct control of the vaccaries dwindled and they farmed them out. With the disafforestation of upland areas, such as Rossendale, the former vaccaries were re-let as copyhold tenancies (Tupling 1927; Cunliffe Shaw 1956, 472–4). The medieval vaccaries thus formed the post-medieval settlement pattern of tenanted individual farmsteads and hamlets (Winchester 1993, 23–7).

Medieval expansion and desertion

The twelfth and thirteenth centuries nationally experienced sustained population growth. The effect was to increase settlement pressure on lands previously regarded as marginal. New areas were taken out of the surviving woodland and waste. These assarts resulted in small irregularly-shaped fields sometimes farmed by a newly-sited single farmstead. Assarts are recorded as being made on the slopes of Longridge Fell from the early thirteenth century (*ibid*). Between 1241 and 1258, on lands held by the manor of Burnley, hundreds of acres within Forest were assarted for agriculture and eight cottages erected (Cunliffe Shaw 1956, 437). Parts of the mosses were drained and new settlements appeared. By 1296 a hamlet called Mosshouses had been established on the mires edge near Much Hoole (Winchester 1993, 17). There is some evidence to suggest that moated sites formed part of a thirteenth century expansion in settlement into the mosslands. An example of such a site maybe the moat at Pasture Barn, near Medlar, found during the North West Wetland Survey (Middleton *et al* 1995, 116, 240). At Risley, now in Cheshire, a thirteenth century moated site which seems to be a moosland assart has been recently excavated (LUAU 1996).

Settlement desertions went on throughout the Middle Ages, for example the Domesday township of *Aschebi* in Amounderness may have disappeared because it was incorporated into an area under Forest Law (Kenyon 1991, 171), but it is only with widespread population contraction that desertions became common. In the fourteenth century the increased population collapsed. This was a European-wide phenomenon, in part brought about by the plague pandemic known as the Black Death. In the later fourteenth century it is estimated that the population may have declined by 30%–50%. A decline in the population offered opportunities to the survivors, poor holdings and tenancies could be abandoned for newly available more favourable ones. Hence the more marginal, less favoured sites tended to be abandoned.

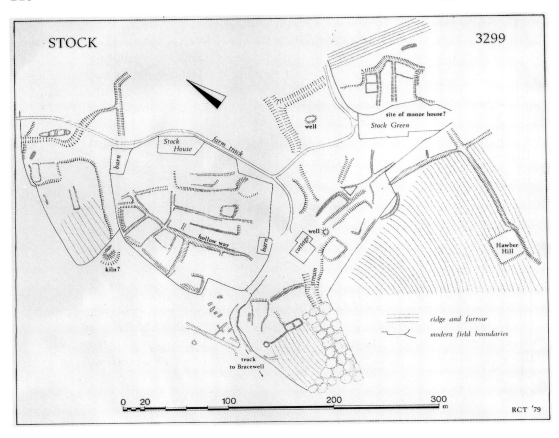

Plan of medieval settlement earthworks at Stock, near Barnoldswick

How important plague was in depopulation in medieval Lancashire, one of the less populous areas of England, is debateable. Famine may have been a more frequent generator of excessive mortality than plague in Lancashire (Platt 1996, 35).

The most noticeable sites to be affected by settlement shrinkage are the largest, so it is the nucleated settlements which appear to have been most affected by contraction. There are a number of possible deserted or shrunken nucleated settlements in the lowland zone such as Mythop and Medlar in Amounderness, and in the woodland frontier zone settlements like Yealand Storrs, near the Westmorland border. Within this zone, in the Lancashire part of the former West Riding of Yorkshire, is a particular concentration of deserted medieval nucleated sites, including Battersby, Easington, and Stock, the latter being the most impressive set of medieval settlement earthworks in the county. Some of these sites maybe the result of settlement shifting rather than depopulation. Settlement shifting may explain the dense medieval pottery scatters

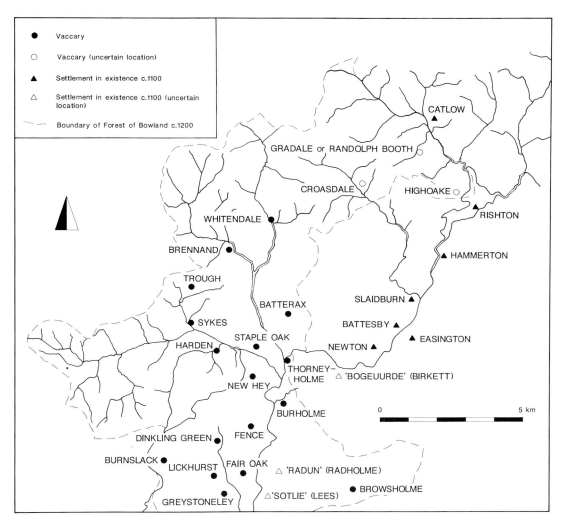

Map of vaccaries in Bowland

noted around Inskip in Amounderness, though these may be the remains of middens as suggested by the North West Wetlands Survey team (Middleton *et al* 1995, 116). There is no doubt that individual farmsteads are underrepresented in the record of deserted sites. Nevertheless, the lack of deserted farmstead sites could be a reflection of a real lack of late medieval desertions of this type of site, particularly in the uplands. The vaccary system may have acted against site desertion. The vaccaries of Bowland for example show little evidence for upland site abandonment between the early fourteenth and fifteenth centuries (Cunliffe Shaw 1956; Higham 1978).

The research agenda

Virtually all of this paper has been concerned with hypotheses derived from documentary sources. This is a fair reflection of the significance of the contribution of archaeology, particularly the recovery of below ground remains, to the understanding of medieval rural settlement in Lancashire. Few sites have been investigated scientifically or systematically. Those recent sites which have been examined, such as the deserted village site at Rufford, or Freckleton and Broughton moats, have either been investigated in the context of modern conservation-led archaeology — the object of which is the prevention of damage rather then the acquisition of knowledge — and/or have proved to be elusive in character.

Our knowledge of moated sites is much better than our knowledge of other settlement types, but they have received so much attention because of their visibility. They are not crucial to the understanding of Lancashire's medieval settlement evolution. Attention should be focused away from specific sites and toward wider landscapes in which the interaction of nucleated and dispersed settlement patterns, lowland and upland, village/hamlet, and farmstead can be studied. In particular we need to investigate the chronologies of both nucleated and dispersed sites.

Specific research questions include:

- when, where, and why did nucleation take place;

- did the nucleations result from a coalescence of earlier foci or did they occur on wholly new sites;

- what is the evidence for continuity from earlier periods;

- what was the nature of the cultural and environmental factors that produced the settlement pattern mappable in the post-medieval period;

- how were settlements affected by, and effect, change within their local environments;

- how did the vernacular building tradition develop and what does it suggest about social organisation and development;

- how did the vaccary farmstead sites evolve and what is the material culture associated with the vaccaries.

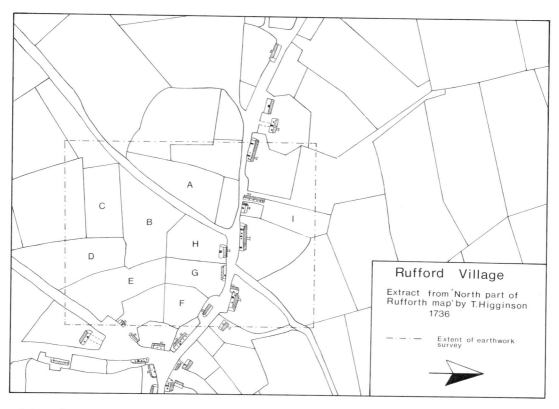

Map of Rufford village in 1736. A village of medieval origin in the post-medieval period

There are many other questions which can be asked, particularly concerning economy and environment, none of which should have answers sought site specifically but should be examined within a wider perspective. It is essential that the sites are investigated in the context of their townships and that the regional relationships of the township, are examined. As for vaccaries, not only should the main farm site be investigated but any dependant sites should also be examined. In order to explore these issues there are associated matters, in particular the need to resolve problems relating to local pottery manufacture and distribution and the relative chronologies constructed around these artefacts. Not only are excavations of rural settlements and production sites required to do this, but a local type series needs to be started on the basis of existing assemblages (Mellor 1994, 68). Overall inter-disciplinary researches are needed to study the interaction and evolution of settlements within their landscapes (Austin 1989, 245–6a).

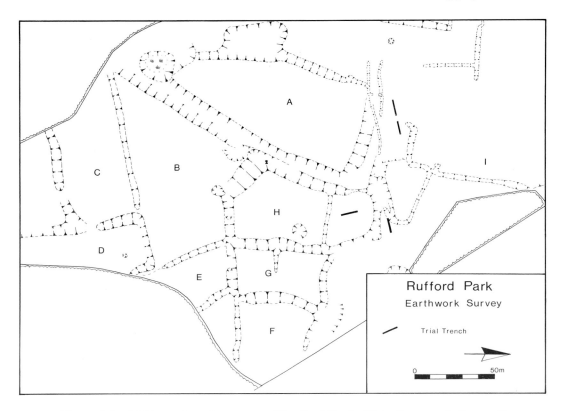

Plan of the 1991 earthwork survey of Rufford Park. Note the correlation with boundaries on the 1736 map

The difficulties of excavating such sites should not be forgotten. Chief amongst these is the problem of recognition. The surviving material culture of a site's earlier phases is likely to be sparse and possibly undatable. The potentially ephemeral nature of the remains, even those dating to the thirteenth-fourteenth centuries, has been highlighted by LUAU's recent excavation at Fazakerley (LUAU 1995). In order to tease out worthwhile data, such sites require well designed research strategies, carefully targeted and often extensive excavations, undertaken in good weather conditions and supported by an appropriate range of modern scientific resources.

This research agenda has highlighted excavation. In these conservation-minded days this is not fashionable, but whilst other methods may detect sites, below ground investigations are required to explain them. Excavation provides the opportunity to clarify settlement morphology, and the development of building plans and forms (Austin 1989a, 241), moreover, through the analysis of artefacts in particular they give the chance to get closer to the people who built and lived in them. Excavations cannot be undertaken in isolation but must form part of interdisciplinary projects, utilising geophysical investigation, palaeoenvironmental sampling, fieldwalking, documentary research, morphological analysis, and survey. Indeed survey is urgently needed in the uplands to identify sites as a preliminary to any detailed investigation. The research agenda posed seeks answers to very basic questions, which in other areas may have been answered already allowing research interests to move on (see Austin 1990), but in Lancashire the initial groundwork is still required. Our database is deficient and requires updating. At present it is biased toward the highly visible, unwittingly exaggerating the importance of certain site types, and focusing attention on failed nucleated settlements and moated sites, which were just a part of the complex kaleidoscope of shifting patterns and relationships which characterised Lancashire's medieval rural settlement history.

References

Astill, G, 1988 Rural settlement: the toft and the croft, in *The countryside of medieval England* (eds G Astill and A Grant), Oxford, 36–61

Aston, M, Austin, D, and Dyer, C, 1989 *The rural settlements of medieval England*, Oxford

Atkin, M A, 1985 Some settlement patterns in Lancashire, in *Medieval Villages* (ed D Hooke), Oxford Univ Comm Archaeol Monogr, **5**, Oxford, 170–185

Austin, D, 1989a The excavation of dispersed settlement in medieval Britain, in *The rural settlements of medieval England*, (by M Aston, D Austin, and C Dyer), Oxford, 231–246

Austin, D, 1989b Medieval settlement in the North East of England — retrospect, summary, and prospect, in *Medieval rural settlement in North East England* (ed B E Vyner), Architect Archaeol Soc Durham Northumberland Res Rep **2**, Durham, 141–150

Austin, D, 1990 The 'proper study' of medieval archaeology, in *From the Baltic to the Black Sea* (eds D Austin and L Alcock), London, 9–42

Bagley, J J, 1976 *A history of Lancashire*, 6th edn, Chichester and London

Higham, M, 197 The -erg place-names of Northern England, *Journ English Place-Name Soc*, **10**, 7–17

Higham, M, 1991 The mottes of North Lancashire, Lonsdale, and South Cumbria, *Trans Cumberland Westmorland Antiq Archaeol Soc*, **91**, 79–90

Hoskins, W G, 1955 *The making of the English landscape*, London

Kenyon, D, 1991 *The origins of Lancashire*, Manchester

LUAU, 1995 *Higher Lane, Fazakerley, Merseyside: assessment of evaluation and of excavation*, unpubl client report

LUAU, 1996 *Old Abbey Farm, Risley, Cheshire: an archaeological assessment report*, unpubl client report

Mellor, M, 1994 *Medieval ceramic studies in England: a review for English Heritage*, London

Middleton, R, Wells, C E, and Huckerby, E, 1995 *The wetlands of North Lancashire*, North West Wetlands Survey, **3**, Lancaster Imprints, **4**, Lancaster

Platt, C, 1996 *King Death: The Black Death and its aftermath in late-medieval England*, London

Fishwick, H, Lieut-Col., 1879 *Lancashire and Cheshire Surveys 1649–1655*. The Record Society for the Publication of Original Documents relating to Lancashire and Cheshire

Roberts, B, 1972 Village plans in County Durham: a preliminary statement, *Med Archaeol*, **16**, 33–56

Roberts, B, 1987 *The making of the English village*, Singapore

Roberts, B, 1990 Back lanes and tofts, distribution maps, and time, medieval nucleated settlement in the north of England, in *Medieval rural settlement in North East England* (ed B E Vyner), Architect Archaeol Soc Durham Northumberland Res Rep, **2**, Durham, 107–125

Shaw, R C, 1956 *The Royal Forest of Lancaster*, Preston

Taylor, C, 1983 *Village and farmstead*, London

Tupling, G H, 1927 *The economic history of Rossendale*, Chetham Soc, New Ser, **86**, Manchester

Walker, F, 1939 *Historical geography of South West Lancashire before the Industrial Revolution*, Chetham Soc, New Ser, **103**, Manchester, 5

Winchester, A, 1993 Field, wood, and forest — landscapes of medieval Lancashire in *Lancashire local studies* (ed A Crosby), Preston, 7–27

8

MEDIEVAL TOWNS

by Andrew White

Medieval Lancashire had no cities and very few towns. One is forced to the conclusion that it was not a very important area economically at that time, compared for instance with East Anglia. This situation may have been compounded by the effects of border warfare. Although Lancashire was directly affected on only two occasions by Scottish invasion, in 1322 and in 1389, the threat must have hung over the region for several centuries, dissuading landowners or citizens from investing heavily in buildings or property. The county itself was of relatively late origins — it did not exist at the time of the Domesday Survey — and as late as the mid-twelfth century the northern part was ceded to Scotland during the troubles of the Anarchy (Kenyon 1991). The picture changed utterly after the Industrial Revolution, of which Lancashire was one of the cradles, but that is another story. The effects of the Industrial Revolution, however, shroud the earlier townscapes. We need to look through the veil of later development in order to see the nature and pattern of earlier urban settlement.

Very few Lancashire towns have seen any archaeological excavation at all. Those excavations aimed specifically at finding the answer to questions raised by their medieval development are even fewer. Some excavations aimed at solving quite different problems have incidentally uncovered medieval information, but rarely on a scale sufficient to satisfy medievalists. For instance, we have not yet defined archaeologically a single burgage plot or a single medieval house site in any Lancashire town. The Domesday evidence suggests that towns were not a characteristic feature of the area before the Conquest and may have been largely a product of the Norman economy, though proto-urban defended sites may have been established in the tenth century at Penwortham and Lancaster (Crosby 1994). This theory remains to be tested archaeologically.

It must be said that with the coming of developer-funding for archaeological excavation, so work is almost entirely limited to that made necessary by urban redevelopment. Consequently the likelihood of gaining answers to the research questions medievalists would pose is greatly diminished. Looked at in another and more positive light, there are strong reasons for setting priorities for each town, balancing the questions we would like to answer with the sites to which we are likely

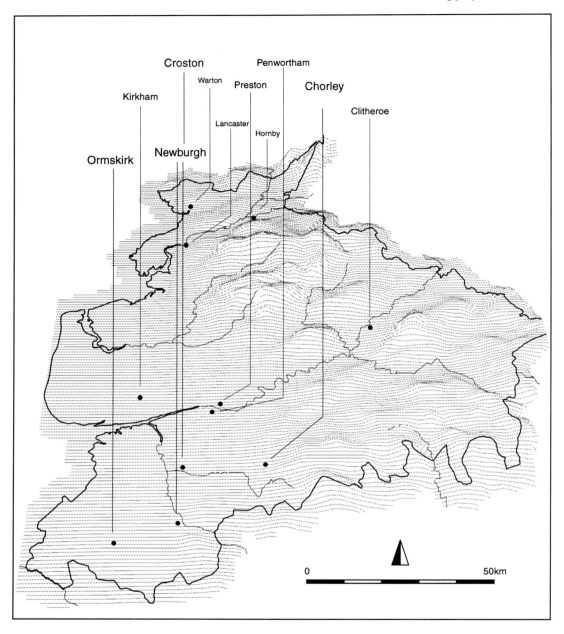

Medieval boroughs in Lancashire

to gain access in the foreseeable future. Some of these priorities remain surprisingly unchanged from the agenda set in 1972 in *The erosion of history* (Heighway 1972).

Post-medieval change

Lancashire has been changed more than almost any other county by the Industrial Revolution, and most of its urban roots lie within it. A whole series of towns along the coast — Lytham, Blackpool, Fleetwood, and Morecambe — represent an even later origin, based on the Victorian discovery of the seaside. In the Middle Ages these towns were represented by tiny fishing hamlets (Bagley 1967, 64–5). Many of what are now the county's largest inland towns were represented in the Middle Ages by villages or hamlets. In the case of Accrington, recorded as 'depopulated' when it became a grange of Kirkstall Abbey, the settlement practically disappeared during the Middle Ages (Beresford 1954, 359). Others, like Blackburn and Burnley, though larger, were arguably not urban in character and did not govern themselves as boroughs. Of course there were a number of thriving medieval towns in England which were not boroughs; such towns which remained wholly in the control of a lord, but Lancashire's larger villages do not seem to fit into this category.

Chartered Boroughs

This leaves only a few ancient boroughs marked by distinctive rights granted by charter, usually including those of market and fair as well as freedom from the lord's service, in return for a cash payment. Towns such as Lancaster and Preston gained such charters in the late twelfth century (Beresford and Finberg 1973, 131–5). Whether there was any sort of urban settlement here before the granting of their respective charters is open to question. It has become fashionable to push 'urban' origins back beyond the earliest charters, on the grounds that landlords were in effect accepting a *fait accompli* in their grants of charter rights. This is one of the points which archaeology might settle. At Sleaford, Lincolnshire, for instance, a town previously thought to be a thirteenth century planting by the Bishop of Lincoln, archaeological excavation in the Market Place conclusively demonstrated evidence of much earlier settlement, requiring a reappraisal of the historical evidence. It may be that there were already proto-towns of Lancaster, Preston, Clitheroe, etc, lacking borough status and chartered market rights, but awaiting the right economic and legal stimulus to be called into being. The earliest borough charters and the earliest corroborative documents such as monastic cartularies both belong to the late twelfth century, so we have no independent documentary evidence (such as that of street names) before the granting of borough status to help us with this problem.

Most of the other boroughs were created in the early and mid-thirteenth century. Some, like Hornby and Warton, would scarcely now be thought urban although they

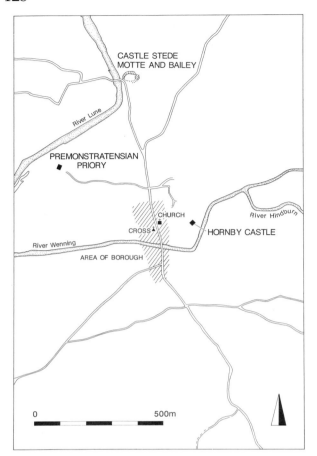

Hornby: location plan and detail plan showing the features of a typical seigniorial borough which was fostered in the late 13th century, and was in decay by the late Middle Ages.

acquired charters and burgesses in the Middle Ages. Some of the seeds of this medieval sowing of towns simply failed to germinate, either because they were in the wrong place or because they were sown at the wrong time. Nonetheless there may remain residual elements of urban character even in these failed towns. Hornby is a classic example of a 'seigniorial borough' — a borough planted by a great magnate — and though some of these elements are now vestigial it had a castle, a chapel, a market place with a cross, and tollbooth, and a grammar school, as well as a priory endowed by the medieval lords of Hornby (White 1985–6, 1–7).

There is some evidence that the Nevilles, who created the borough, moved a pre-existing settlement from the vicinity of Castle Stede, the earthwork castle they had inherited, to a more satisfactory site beside the River Wenning. They were even able to put forward a convincing challenge to Lancaster's market rights which the older borough had difficulty in fighting off, because these rights were implicit rather than explicit in the earliest charters (Pape 1952, 23–4). Such arguments over market rights may well have helped to space out urban centres to the ten and twenty mile distances so familiar even today. In 1487–8, and clearly much earlier, Lancaster was using its market rights to claim passage tolls on goods passing along the busy road linking West Yorkshire with Cumbria (now the A65) at Cowan Bridge, fifteen miles away (Brownbill and Nuttall 1929, 15). Such lucrative rights were guarded jealously.

Lancaster and Preston, along with Liverpool, Manchester, Wigan, and Warrington represented the larger chartered towns of historical Lancashire by the mid-thirteenth century, although 'large' is a relative word for populations in the bracket of one to three thousand: estimates of settlement population at this time are difficult to arrive at, and sometimes represent parochial, rather than township, figures. Today such sites would be considered village-like in their density of population. Others, such as Clitheroe, were even smaller but at a convenient distance from larger centres so that they were not in direct competition. We know that Clitheroe had 66 burgesses in 1258 which is not much more than Hornby with 47 ½ in 1319 (Beresford and Finberg 1973, 131–2). Half a burgage (or a burgess for that matter!) does not make a great deal of sense; it is likely that the reference is to a moiety of a larger figure, the records of which are now lost.

Wealth and prosperity

One measure of prosperity in the Middle Ages can be called 'the Friary test'. The various orders of friars were mendicants; they owned little property and relied upon the generosity of townsfolk for their living. By the middle of the thirteenth century they were very widely spread but the largest houses, and widest range of orders, were to be found in the most prosperous towns and cities. London, Oxford, Cambridge, York, Newcastle, and Norwich contained the most houses of friars, with between five and seven orders each (Knowles and Hadcock 1971; Midmer 1979). This very much reflects the size and importance of these cities — Oxford and Cambridge were also important educationally to the friars. Chester, Lancashire's nearest city, had three houses of friars. By contrast only three Lancashire towns had any friaries at all. These were Lancaster with Dominicans, Preston with Franciscans, and Warrington with Austins. There were many reasons for their arrival, success, or failure in particular places, but in general they could only survive where there was sufficient surplus for the townsfolk to support their parasitic growth. Therefore, the presence of a friary is a useful index of prosperity. It may be significant that all three towns were on the main road to the north and so the alms of travellers eaked out the meagre alms of the townsfolk.

Another measure is the set of statistics which can be drawn from the Lay Subsidy of 1334. Glasscock (1975) produced a series of bandings of relative wealth from this to show how rich or otherwise various localities were. This is not without its problems since a relatively wealthy urban area could be brought down in the overall league table by being counted with a thinly-populated rural area. Preston emerges on various counts as the most prosperous town, paying more tax to the king in 1227 than either Lancaster or Liverpool. The recent Scottish invasion of 1322 was not without its effects upon Lancashire towns. Two armies under the Earl of Murray and Lord James Douglas met at Lancaster (Holinshed 1808, V, 355) and stayed there for four days in late August. After looting and burning the town the Scots moved on to Preston, and perhaps as far as Chorley and repeated the performance. At Lancaster the evidence of destruction appears in the Inquest taken the following year when values of a number of properties are set at nil or greatly reduced. (Farrer 1907, 115–126). To date no archaeological evidence for this event has been produced.

Seigniorial boroughs

We have already seen the relationship between town and Friary in the Middle Ages. Clitheroe, Hornby, Lancaster, Liverpool, Penwortham, and Warrington are all associated with castles, in most cases those of the very lords who gave them their borough charters. Not all the castles survived as seigniorial strong points, however. The castles at Penwortham and of Warrington were motte and bailey castles, abandoned fairly early. Penwortham, indeed, is the only borough to appear in the Domesday entries relating to Lancashire (Morgan 1978, 270, a, b) and seems to have been replaced soon afterwards by Preston with its better site. In 1086 it had only six burgesses and appears to have been a recent creation. Such a site, the urban character of which was only incipient, would be a valuable candidate for archaeological examination like those monasteries (*see* Wood *below*) which were abandoned before they had fully developed. At Hornby the motte and bailey at Castle Stede, close to the river Lune, was likewise abandoned in favour of a better site above the River Wenning about a mile away, and it was below this that the new town was laid out on the road between Lancaster and Kirkby Lonsdale at some time soon after 1279.

Monastic boroughs

Abbeys also played their part in the founding of boroughs, such as Vale Royal at Kirkham in 1296 and Burscough Priory at Ormskirk ten years earlier. As with lay landlords their purpose was profit; it was regarded as more profitable to foster a free borough than to retain the inhabitants as conventional manorial tenants, and the thirteenth century was a period of confidence, economic growth, and rapid urban development. Even in the other towns established by lay landlords monastic corporations such as Cockersand and Furness Abbeys held considerable interests and their properties are among the best documented, providing us with much incidental information.

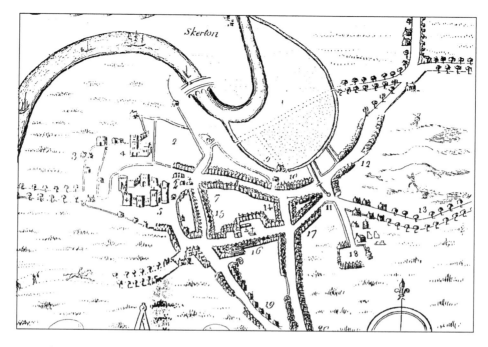

John Speed's map of Lancashire 1610 includes in one corner a plan of
Lancaster, which is the earliest plan of the town in existence. It shows a town
which had changed in few material aspects since the Middle Ages; even the Dominican
Friary retains the ruins of its buildings

Town plans

Later maps, especially those of the seventeenth century, can be a useful source for examining and identifying areas and streets which existed in the Middle Ages. The layout of burgage plots, the position and size of the market place, and the relationship with parish church or castle can be determined from the best of the pre-Ordnance Survey town plans — not necessarily from the oldest (Conzen 1968, 113–30). Both Lancaster and Preston are very fortunate in having accurate large-scale plans made in 1684 which show individual properties in detail. The survey sheets were found at Towneley Hall in the early 1950s and are now in the Lancashire Record Office (DDX/194). These studies are not only the preserve of archaeologists: sociologists and historical geographers use similar evidence, but the questions they ask, and the methods they employ for answering them, can be quite different. Indeed the archaeological solutions will generally give specific snapshots of individual properties rather than an overview, but carefully placed excavations or even a sequence of watching briefs may help to indicate more general trends.

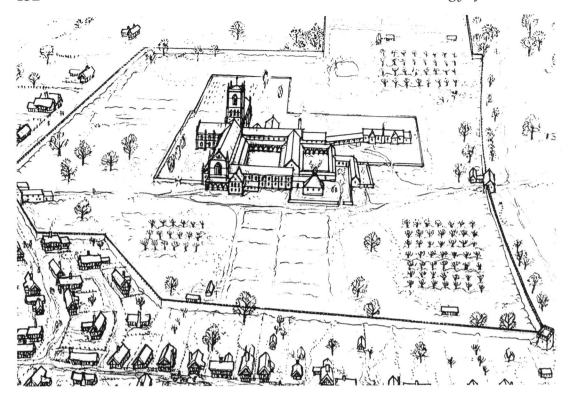

Lancaster's Dominican Friary in the early 16th century,
(by Andrew White and David Vale)

Archaeological excavations

Of all these towns mentioned, very few have seen any archaeological excavation and even fewer have had work aimed at answering specific questions about the Middle Ages. Lancaster, Preston, and Warrington have had the most work done. The small towns and failed boroughs have had the least attention; unfortunately a potentially interesting site at Warton, examined in 1986, failed to produce any archaeology at all.

In Lancaster excavations in the Vicarage Fields have located the precinct wall of the Priory and a gatehouse in it (White 1988, 8–12). In China Street sites of two post-medieval houses have been investigated. It is suggested that China Street was not one of the oldest streets, but had been slipped in between existing burgage plots (Penney 1980, 3–33;1981, 18). In Church Street many medieval rubbish pits and traces of industrial processes were found on the site of the old Brewery, including the greatest quantity of medieval pottery yet found in Lancaster (Newman *et al* forthcoming).

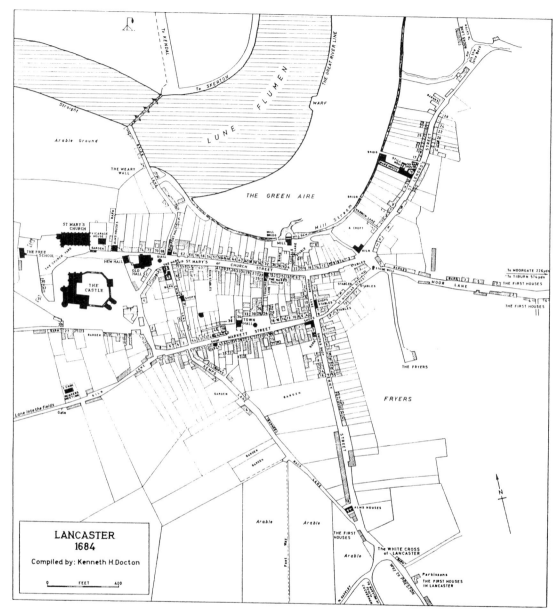

Lancaster in 1684 (redrawn by Kenneth Docton)

ALMS HOUSES

FISHERGATE

FRIARGATE

MARKET
PLACE

ST JOHN'S
CHURCH

SCHOOL

WINDMILL

CHURCH STREET

ALMS HOUSES

0   200m

Preston in 1684 (redrawn by Dick Danks)

Probable medieval well found during excavations at the Mitchells Brewery site, Lancaster

Finally, some work has been done on the Dominican Friary in Sulyard Street, though most of the evidence was found during the nineteenth century (Penney 1982, 1–6). The biggest and most obvious omission is any detailed work in the immediate area of the medieval Priory, or within the walls of the Castle. While some work on the standing fabric of the latter is now under way, and some limited excavations have been undertaken near to the gatehouse (LUAU 1995), it will require a major change in the Castle's use — it is presently a functioning prison — to allow excavations within the courtyard or even at selected points on the outside of the walls.

In Preston much less has been done. In 1980 excavations took place in Church Street; although the site occupied three medieval burgage plots cellaring and other disturbances had removed all but the bases of pits (Youngs and Clark 1981, **25**, 209). In 1989 work was undertaken on a site in Fishergate. Here again only rubbish pits survived but a good sample of medieval pottery was recovered on this occasion (Gaimster *et al* 1990, **36**, 199). Excavations on the site of the friary in 1991 were similarly disappointing as far as the structural evidence went, since it appeared that later industrial uses had destroyed all the conventual buildings thought to lie in that area and only medieval pottery and fragments of floor-tiles were recovered (Nenk *et al* 1992, **36**, 247; Tostevin and Iles 1991–2, 62–7).

In Warrington, as at Lancaster, most interest had focused upon the Roman remains. However, significant work has been carried out on the motte and bailey castle and upon the Austin Friary, leading to the discovery of a large part of its plan. Most of this work was carried out in the nineteenth century and its archaeological value is slight, although large areas of floor-tiles were recovered (Owen 1889, 175–94). More recent excavations in Friars' Gate in 1978 located the cemetery of the Friary.

What has been done takes little time to record. What needs to be done has yet to be determined by the careful consideration of a number of specialists. As the remainder of this volume shows clearly there are a number of overlaps between period or subject interests. The following, however, is a personal interim list of the issues.

Research agenda

Burgage plots: we lack the history of even a single burgage plot, where the medieval levels survive, in any Lancashire town.

Market places: the history of the market place is a particularly important element of any town. At Lancaster it is thought that Market Street and Market Square may be creations of the 1193 borough charter (White 1993,26).

Development of the street pattern: this can be studied by non-archaeological means but some testing of critical points and junctions would resolve a number of problems. The street plan of central Preston is not at all complex but even here there seems to be *prima facie* evidence for growth and change in the medieval period.

Urban origins: we lack any detailed knowledge of whether the new boroughs were as new as they seem, how they were altered in terms of layout to meet their new role if not, or what they had looked like beforehand.

Smaller seigniorial boroughs: no work has yet been carried out in any of these. Specific questions should be posed in each case.

Urban friaries: quite apart from their own significance, the friaries mirror the wealth and aspirations of the townspeople and since they were dissolved by 1540 they provide a very useful cut-off point before post-medieval development took place.

Urban industry: we know little of the industrial processes carried out, although the medieval monastic cartularies are full of references to urban industry.

Medieval pottery sequence: reasonable samples are now known from Lancaster and Preston but without a detailed sequence we shall never be able to sort out the complex dating of urban structures when they emerge. No significant medieval groups have yet been published for any Lancashire town (Davey 1977, 108, 121; McCarthy and Brooks 1988).

In addition to the above priorities there are non-excavational considerations such as determining which areas need to be further protected from damage or destruction by scheduling, conservation-area status, or other planning procedures.

References

Bagley, J J, 1967 *A history of Lancashire*, 4th edn, London and Chichester

Beresford, M W, 1969 *The lost villages of England* , London

Beresford, M W, and Finberg, H P R, 1973 *English medieval boroughs, a handlist*, Newton Abbot

Best, D, 1988 *A short history of Clitheroe in Lancashire*, Preston

Brownbill, J, and Nuttall, J R, 1929 *A calendar of charters and records belonging to the Corporation of Lancaster*, Lancaster

Conzen, M R G, 1968 The use of town plans in the study of urban history, in *The study of urban history* (ed H J Dyos), Leicester

Crosby, A, 1994 The towns of medieval Lancashire: an overview, *CNWRS Regional Bull*, **8**, 7–18

Davey, P J (ed), 1977 *Medieval pottery from excavations in the North West*, Liverpool

Farrer, W, 1907 Lancashire inquests, extents, and feudal aids, Pt II, *Lancashire Cheshire Record Soc*, **54**, 115–126

Gainster, D R M, Margeson, S, and Hurley, M, 1990 Medieval Britain and Ireland in 1989, *Medieval Archaeology*, **34**, 162–252

Glasscock, R E (ed), 1975 The Lay-Subsidy of 1334, *Rec Social Economic Hist*, 149–56

Hunt, D, 1992 *A history of Preston*, Preston

Heighway, C M, 1972 *The erosion of history; archaeology and planning in towns*, CBA 60–63, London 78–81

Holinshed, R, 1808 *Holinshed's chronicle of England, Scotland, and Ireland*, **5**, 355

Kenyon, D, 1991 *The origins of Lancashire*, Manchester

Knowles, M D, and Hadcock, R N, 1971 *Medieval religious houses, England and Wales*, Harlow

McCarthy, M R, and Brooks, C M, 1988 *Medieval pottery in Britain AD 900–1600*, Leicester

Midmer, R, 1979 *English medieval monasteries 1066–1540*, London

Morgan, P (ed), 1978 *Domesday Book; Cheshire*, Chichester

Morris, M, 1983 *Medieval Manchester; a regional study*, Manchester

Nenk, S, Margerson, S, and Hurley, M, 1992 Medieval Britain and Ireland in 1991, *Medieval Archaeology*, **36**, 184–308

Newman, R, in prep *Excavations in Lancaster 1988 and 1992*

Owen, W, 1889 Warrington Friary — recent discoveries, *Hist Soc Lancashire Cheshire Trans*, **41**, 175–94

Pape, T, 1952 *The charters of the City of Lancaster*, Lancaster

Penney, S H, 1980 The excavation of two post-medieval houses in China Street, Lancaster, 1979, *Contrebis*, **8**, 3–33

Penney, S H, 1981 *Lancaster: the evolution of its townscape to 1800*, CNWRS Occas Paper, **9**, Lancaster

Penney, S H, 1982 Excavations at Lancaster Friary 1980–81, *Contrebis*, **10**, 1–6

Tostevin, P, and Iles, P, 1991/2 Preston Friary — an archaeological evaluation, *Contrebis*, **17**, 62–7

White, A J, 1985–6 Some notes on medieval Hornby, *Contrebis*, **12**, 1–7

White, A J, 1988 Did Lancaster Priory have a precinct wall?, *Contrebis*, **14**, 8–12

White, A J (ed), 1993 *A history of Lancaster 1193–1993*, Keele

Youngs, S M, and Clark, J, 1981 Medieval Britain in 1980, *Medieval Archaeology*, **25**, 166–228

9

CASTLES AND MONASTERIES

by Jason Wood

The principal aim of this paper is to examine potential research frameworks for the study of Lancashire's castles and monasteries in the medieval and post-medieval periods. Those castles and monasteries which lie outside the limits of the modern administrative area of Lancashire will be excluded. Sites in the former West Riding of Yorkshire, which now forms part of Lancashire, are included.

Past studies of Lancashire's castles and monasteries have been undertaken mainly by historians and antiquarians in the earlier part of this century. There has been no serious attempt to examine the sites as a group, and there is no Royal Commission volume for the county. General source material must therefore be our starting point. Any study of castles has to begin with reference to King's *Castellarium Anglicanum* (1983) and for the monastic sites there is Knowles and Hadcock's *Medieval Religious Houses – England and Wales* (2nd edition, 1971). Site specific references will not be given in the following text but details are contained in the general works cited above, and in the relevant entries in the county's Sites and Monuments Record.

Lancashire's castles

Of the county's earthwork castles, King lists seven extant (Arkholme, Gisburn (Castle Haugh), Halton, Hornby (Castlestede), Melling, Penwortham, and Whittington); two vanished (Preston (Tulketh) and Mourhall (Warton)); and one possible (Borwick). Higham (1991) has since made a stronger case for Borwick and suggested a further three (Dolphinholme, Ellenthorpe, and Whitewell). In addition, it is possible that the masonry castles at Clitheroe and Lancaster had earthwork predecessors. King lists five extant masonry castles (Clitheroe, Greenhalgh, Hornby, Lancaster, and Thurland); and one vanished castle (Lathom House). Two extant masonry towers (Borwick Hall and Turton) and one vanished tower (Broughton) are also considered.

It is generally agreed that the first earthwork castles are a Norman phenomenon, and are usually dated to the eleventh and early twelfth centuries. In Lancashire there is a

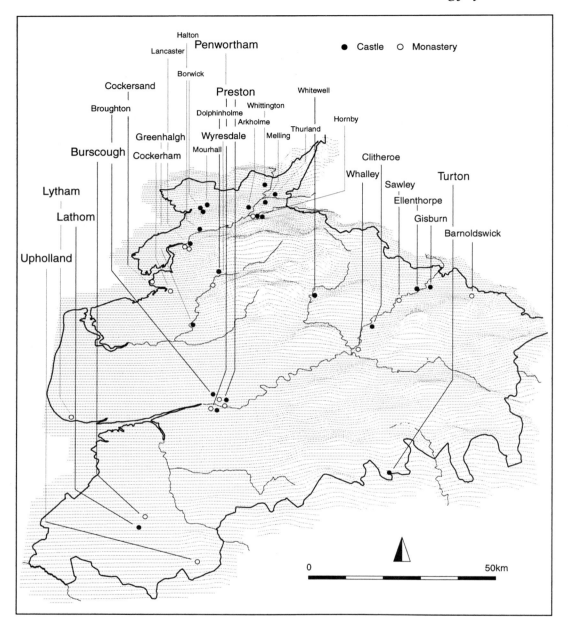

Castles and monasteries mentioned in the text

Aerial view of the earthwork castle at Halton

recognisable grouping of mottes in the northern half of the county, particularly concentrating on the valleys of the Lune and Ribble. From the mid-late twelfth century, and with the abandonment of the earthwork sites and construction of the first masonry castles, it would appear that centralised administration was becoming based on a smaller number of prestige sites. The largest of these was at Lancaster where the earliest standing fabric is found in the keep. This large and imposing stone tower is traditionally attributed to Roger of Poitou (before 1102), but if so, the keep would be the third oldest in England. It is more likely that Roger's castle was a simple earthwork construction. The structure resembles many keeps built in the middle years of the twelfth century, and it has been suggested that its construction was initiated by David I of Scotland, who is known to have ordered extensive building at Carlisle, probably on the keep there. Clitheroe, built by the de Lacy family, is not reliably attested before 1186 but the keep (one of the smallest in England) probably dates to the 1170s. Again earlier mentions in 1102 and 1123–24 would suggest an earthwork predecessor.

The early thirteenth century (1208–11) saw work on the castle ditch at Lancaster, and perhaps a hall and parts of the curtain wall and towers. Other towers and part of the curtain — including the extant Witches' Tower — were probably added in the mid-late thirteenth century. There is a thirteenth-century tower at Hornby (first mentioned 1205), though the nature and extent of other remains is uncertain.

The tower at Borwick Hall is probably fourteenth century, as was that at Broughton, although the latter is not mentioned until 1515. These towers, like the great number of similar sites further north, particularly in the Morecambe Bay area, would appear to have been built as a response to Scottish raids in the years following Bannockburn in 1314–22.

A feature of Lancashire's castles is the unusually large amount of very late building. Shortly after Henry IV's accession, an extensive rebuilding programme was started at Lancaster, culminating in the construction of the great twin-towered gatehouse

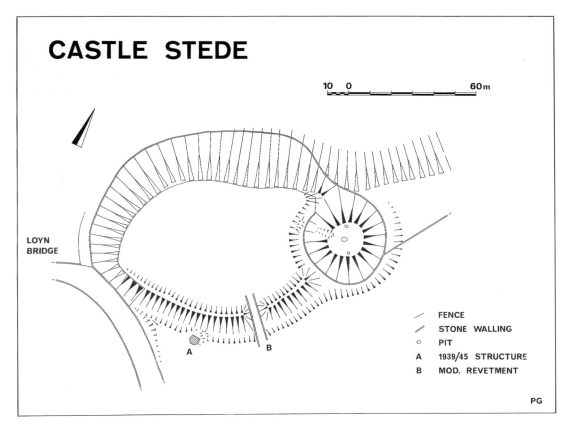

Topographic plan of the earthwork castle at Hornby (Castlestede)

(1403–13) and a recently identified refurbishment of the Witches' Tower. Early fifteenth-century work was apparently carried out at Thurland (licensed 1402), while Greenhalgh (licensed 1490) and the massive Lathom House (1459–95) were both substantial castles built in the late fifteenth century. Descriptions of the castle at Lathom, based on contemporary and later accounts, suggest the presence of a moat, two lines of defensive wall, several gates, a large central tower and perhaps as many as eighteen curtain towers. The tower at Turton is probably of similar date, and the thirteenth-century tower at Hornby was much altered in the early sixteenth century. The upper storey of the keep at Lancaster was rebuilt in the reign of Elizabeth (c1585), as was that of the tower at Turton.

During the post-medieval period a number of Lancashire's castles were lost, particularly during the Civil War and its immediate aftermath. Hornby was taken by storm in 1643 and Thurland ruined following a siege in the same year. Lathom House was besieged unsuccessfully in 1643–4, but taken in 1644 and regrettably totally demolished (so much so that its exact location is disputed). Greenhalgh was almost

Nineteenth-century reconstruction of Lathom House
(from J Roby, 1867 Traditions of Lancashire)

View of the keep at Clitheroe Castle

totally destroyed in 1649–50 following a siege. Clitheroe, already partly ruinous in 1608, was ordered to be slighted in 1649 but survived in part. Lancaster was unsuccessfully attacked in 1643 and 1648 and survived until the late eighteenth century when it was substantially modified for use as a court and prison, during which time the medieval curtain and several of the towers were demolished. Hornby, Thurland, and the towers at Borwick Hall and Turton were converted and extended as dwellings. The tower at Broughton was destroyed in *c*1800 and the keep at Clitheroe substantially repaired in the mid-nineteenth century.

Research agenda for castles

There are a number of issues of local and national significance relating to chronology, function, and distribution of castles, which need to be explored. King found the purpose of the dense group of earthwork castles on the lower Lune 'not easy to explain' (King 1983, 243). Higham argues that the mottes along the valley, together with those at the mouth of the Ribble, should be considered from a military viewpoint and in the context of possible attacks from both Scotland and Ireland, adding that the line of Lune mottes 'might well indicate the 'real' frontier zone at the time of Domesday' (Higham 1991, 85). Lott rejects the idea that the location of mottes was due purely to military considerations related to a deliberate policy of defence and strategic control, arguing that the sites can be more easily explained if they are seen in their feudal roles as centres for secular jurisdiction or administration (Lott 1995, 74–5).

It is likely that both hypotheses carry some weight, with the mottes of the new baronial overlords acting as administrative *foci* and those of subtenants either as outposts of administration or placed in strategic positions. Further research into the distribution pattern of mottes may help to elucidate this debate, while recognising that the Palatinate status of the county may have been a significant factor. In particular, further evidence is needed in order to support the notion of a frontier zone. At the moment, there is nothing to equate mottes as existing by the time of Domesday and there is no hard evidence that these mottes were all built at the same time or for the same reason. Excavation at a number of sites, coupled with documentary research to establish ownership and garrison strengths, should throw more light on the subject. In addition, work building on that of Bu'Lock (1970) and the Lune Valley Survey Project should further examine the coincidence of motte sites with pre-conquest remains, as it might seem logical to assume Norman transplantation to a site which was already recognised as a focal point.

Excavation will be required to confirm the date of abandonment of earthwork sites, and also to establish the existence of earthwork predecessors at Lancaster and Clitheroe and provide confirmation of the authenticity of their assumed foundation dates. Dendrochronological analysis of the principal timbers at the base of the keep at Lancaster would certainly help to confirm its construction date and perhaps who initiated the building — was it indeed David I of Scotland?

Because of the later developments at Lancaster, further knowledge of the nature of the curtain wall and towers and layout of the interior could only be gained through targeted excavations, together with documentary research. Investigation of the nature of outworks, including the castle ditch and causeway, could be achieved through limited geophysical survey and trial excavation. The arrangement of the outer wards and defences at Clitheroe would repay further study, and the nature and extent of the medieval fabric at Hornby and Thurland might be revealed through an examination of the later buildings on these sites. A combination of documentary research, topographic survey, and geophysical survey would hopefully define the location and extent of the sites at Greenhalgh and, more importantly, Lathom House. In view of the scale of the castle at Lathom and its contemporary designation as the 'Northern Court', once its location has been identified further investigation would be justified to increase our knowledge about this nationally significant site.

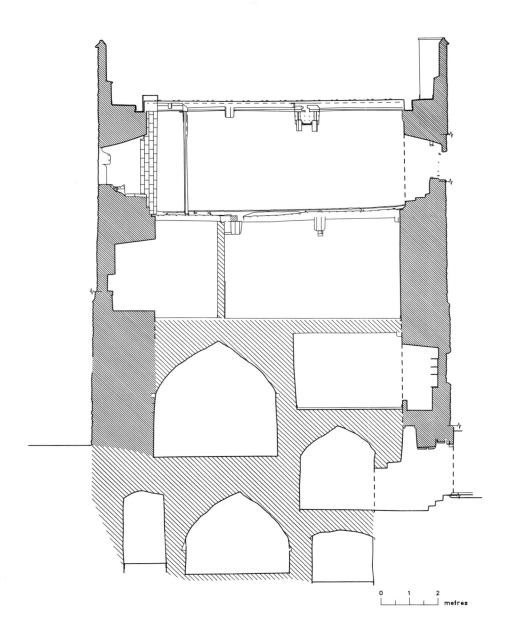

Cross-section through the Witches' Tower at Lancaster Castle

View across Lancaster Castle, showing the keep surrounded by later prison buildings

For all of Lancashire's castles, where sufficient fabric survives, there is a need to establish, through spatial and functional analysis, the layout, access, evolution, and changing function of the constituent parts. With the increasing interest in the non-military uses for castles, research themes could centre on the domestic and social use of these buildings as well as the military.

Tower 'houses' are a particular feature of the North West. As the majority of towers lie to the north of Lancashire, any comparative study of tower chronology, location, design, function, occupation, and decline, together with their manorial history, must be linked to the Cumbrian evidence. Many are today in a neglected condition, often forming redundant parts of still-occupied farms. A straightforward survey for resource management purposes, concentrating on the Morecambe Bay area, might be an appropriate starting point in order to identify recording and conservation priorities.

The post-medieval use of castles should not be neglected. It is necessary to establish the extent of the reuse of the Lancashire castles in the Tudor period and during the Civil War, and also the degree of slighting and rebuilding after the Restoration. Parallel studies of surviving siegeworks relating to the Civil War also should be undertaken. Similarly, it is important to remember that castles are a source for the study of medieval societies and of the landscape they occupied rather than purely military phenomena. Castles were developed within a broader settlement framework and contain evidence extending in its significance far beyond their own physical boundaries.

Lancashire's monasteries

Of the county's known monastic sites, there are six abbeys, three priories, and two friaries. Knowles and Hadcock list three extant abbeys at Cockersand (Premonstratensian), and Sawley (or Sallay), and Whalley (both Cistercian); and three vanished abbeys, namely the early Savigniac site at Preston (Tulketh), and the Cistercian foundations at Barnoldswick and Wyresdale. Extant priories are found at Burscough (Augustinian), and Lancaster and Upholland (both Benedictine). The friaries at Lancaster (Dominican) and Preston (Franciscan) have both vanished, and the evidence for a Franciscan friary at Lancaster is uncertain. In addition, a number of small priories (or cells) and hospitals are known to have existed. Cells were founded at Cockerham (Augustinian), Hornby (Premonstratensian), and Lytham and Penwortham (both Benedictine). Monastic hospitals existed at Burscough, Clitheroe, Cockersand, Hornby, Lancaster (two), Lathom, Preston, and Stidd. There was also a secular college at Upholland. Grange sites are known or postulated at Accrington, Barnoldswick, Beaumont, Burscough (Martin Hall), Morecambe (Poulton), Overton, Rossall, Rushton (now under Stocks reservoir), Staining, Stalmine, and Wrightington (Fairhurst Hall).

Lancashire's first post-Conquest monastery was the Benedictine priory at Lancaster (founded *c*1094), on the site now occupied by St Mary's parish church. The first Savigniac foundation in England was at Preston (Tulketh) and dates from 1124; however, the site was only occupied until 1127 when the monks transferred to Furness. Barnoldswick and Sawley were both founded in 1147, the community at Barnoldswick transferring to Kirkstall (West Yorkshire) in 1152 and the site becoming a grange. Burscough was established by *c*1190 and Cockersand upgraded from a priory to an abbey in *c*1192, having previously been a monastic hospital. The site at Wyresdale was in existence by 1196 but the community transferred to Ireland before 1204. The remains of the church at Sawley date to the late twelfth/early thirteenth century and the chapter house at Cockersand to *c*1230. The Dominican friary at Lancaster and the Franciscan friary at Preston both date to *c*1260. The surviving stump of masonry at Burscough is probably late thirteenth century.

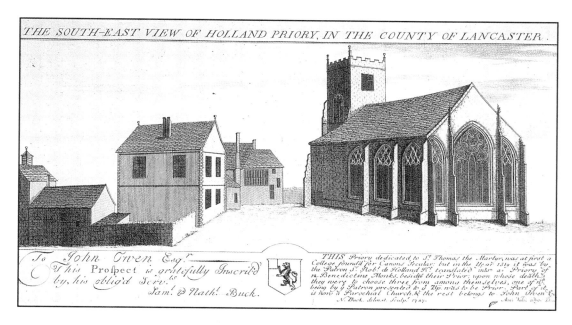

Upholland Priory (from the Buck brothers' print of 1727)

The last monasteries to be built in Lancashire were at Whalley, founded 1296, following the transfer from Stanlaw (Cheshire), and Upholland founded in 1319. At Whalley, fourteenth-century work is recorded on the outer gate (1320) and church (1330–80). The church at Upholland also dates from 1330 and the choir stalls, reputedly from Cockersand (but now at Lancaster), to c1345. A fourteenth-century chapel was added to the church at Sawley.

Work continued at Whalley throughout the fifteenth century. The choir stalls, presumably from the site (but now in the parish church), are early fifteenth, and the claustral buildings, including the abbot's lodging and infirmary, were not finished until the 1440s. The inner gate is even later (c1480). The early sixteenth century saw the construction of a new abbot's lodging and Lady chapel, while at Sawley the church nave was shortened and the presbytery extended.

Between 1536 and 1539, all the Lancashire monasteries were dissolved. Dissolution came early for Lancaster's Benedictine priory. Being an 'alien priory' of Sées in Normandy, the monastic community was disbanded in 1428 during the Hundred Years War with France. The present parish church was built on the site from 1430 and continued as a cell of the Brigittine Convent of Syon until the sixteenth-century suppression. Burscough, Sawley, and Upholland were dissolved in 1536, Whalley in 1537, and Cockersand, Lancaster, and Preston in 1539.

The post-Dissolution history of the sites is varied. At Whalley and the friaries at Lancaster and Preston, parts of the claustral buildings were incorporated into later houses and the remainder of the sites cleared. At Upholland, the presbytery of the priory church was converted to a parish church and some of the claustral buildings reused as a dwelling. The chapter house at Cockersand became a mausoleum but the rest of the site was demolished. Very little survives above ground at Burscough. Late eighteenth- and nineteenth-century redevelopments have completely destroyed both sites at Preston. Twentieth-century repair and conservation works have tended to concentrate on the ruins at Whalley and Sawley.

Research agenda for monasteries

The suggestions put forward below should be seen in the context of the strategies for future research in monastic archaeology outlined by Greene (1992, 227–32; forthcoming).

It would obviously make sense to undertake an audit of existing archaeological documentary archives and to assess such material before exploiting the research potential of the Lancashire monasteries. The three extant abbey sites have all witnessed some level of archaeological excavation in the past two centuries. Whalley was excavated in the 1790s and again in the 1930s, Sawley in the mid-nineteenth century, and Cockersand in the 1920s. Of the vanished monasteries, the area of the precinct and site of the church of the Dominican friary at Lancaster are known from early topographical studies and nineteenth-century excavations.

Very few of these excavation archives have been properly studied or published, and there is a need to critically assess them in relation to more recent work, as at Sawley by the DoE in the early 1980s and at Whalley by LUAU since 1987. An assessment and report on the excavations at Sawley has been recently commissioned by English Heritage as part of the National Backlog Project. Similar consideration of the material from Whalley is essential. LUAU has undertaken no less than ten watching briefs or evaluations and nine different building recording projects at Whalley in less than eight years. The situation is not helped by the fact that the site is in three separate ownerships, and that some parts are scheduled, others listed, and one part (the outer gate) is in State guardianship, resulting in different levels of recording and analysis. Moreover, it houses a functioning but divided religious community, part Roman Catholic, part Anglican. In contrast to Whalley and Sawley, we know little about the sites at Burscough, Cockersand, and Upholland. There is clearly a need for some proactive study or management plan initiative here to assess the nature and extent of

Aerial view of Sawley Abbey, showing the precinct and associated earthworks to the left of the upstanding remains

the remains and to confirm whether the sites are afforded the most appropriate protective status.

The opportunity to excavate an early or temporary monastic site in Lancashire would be of enormous significance for the study of construction techniques for both timber and early stone buildings. The site of the Benedictine priory at Lancaster, where the early layout is unknown, might offer such an opportunity, as would the temporary sites at Barnoldswick and Wyresdale, though the latter is probably now destroyed by a reservoir. In addition, chronological studies of any artifacts recovered from a temporary site would be enhanced, due to such a site's restricted period of use. Unfortunately, the Savigniac foundation at Preston (Tulketh), the forerunner to Furness, was destroyed in the mid-nineteenth century. The temporary occupation of a pre-existing Rectory house and chapel is attested at Whalley, for the period during the initial construction works in the early fourteenth century, while the site at Upholland was occupied by a secular college before the arrival of the priory. An understanding of how these earlier buildings functioned in relation to the growing

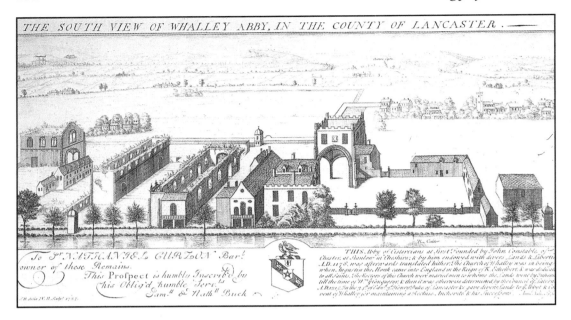

Whalley Abbey (from the Buck brothers' print of 1727)

monasteries would make for an interesting study but later development on the sites may have precluded this.

Comparative studies of the original layouts of monasteries of the different orders, including the mathematics of design, could be a fruitful area for inquiry. For example, accommodation for lay brethren dictated different planning requirements at Cistercian sites, though the need diminished in the later periods. In this respect, the relatively late construction of the West Range building at Whalley, and the early sixteenth-century alterations to the church at Sawley, should provide an opportunity to understand the changing domestic and liturgical arrangements for lay brethren.

Cloisters are among the least understood areas of monastic complexes. Apart from attempting reconstructions from surviving fragments, research could be aimed at establishing the cloister's locational relationship to the surrounding buildings, their internal arrangements relating to drainage and water supply, and the nature of their horticultural use through environmental analysis of soil samples.

The boundaries of monastic precincts and the nature of the ancillary structures within them (for example, mills, barns, bakehouses, brewhouses, fishponds, and dovecots) are of particular interest, especially if related documentation survives. To analyse

View across the remains of Whalley Abbey

these features more aerial photographic and topographic studies of the areas adjacent to monastic sites should be undertaken. There are particularly impressive and extensive earthworks at Sawley, and to a lesser extent at Whalley and Lancaster's Benedictine priory. In Worcestershire, work at Bordesley Abbey has shown how valuable investigations of such areas can be for understanding the economic history of monasteries.

Similarly, a systematic study of grange farms and estate boundaries, through a combination of documentary research, aerial photography, topographic survey, and limited excavation, would considerably enhance our knowledge of the economy of the monastic holdings in the North. The granges at Beaumont and Stalmine were supposedly the two chief granges of Furness in Lonsdale, but there must have been smaller ones as well given the size of the Furness estates.

A study of the nature and extent of the cells and hospitals founded in Lancashire by monasteries further afield, might help to confirm their location and clarify their relationship to the adjacent holdings of the Lancashire sites. The extant, early sixteenth-century remains of the hospital at Lathom would repay further inquiry.

An understanding of the mechanics of the building trade, such as construction logistics and timescales, could be gained from further research into the use of different architectural components within monastic buildings and a systematic study of masons' marks, laying-out lines, and scaffolding and formwork arrangements. Dendrochronological analysis of the choir stalls now at Whalley and Lancaster, combined with a study of their plan and design, would help to clarify their date and supposed provenance.

Because of the Dissolution, most monastic sites have spent at least half their lives, if not more, as ruins and not as buildings in use. It is just as relevant to study, record, and understand the ruined phase of their history as it is their earlier phases. The documentary evidence for the post-Dissolution dispersal of monastic buildings and lands requires collaborative evidence from fieldwork. The utilisation of ruined monastic sites during the picturesque and romantic movements of the late eighteenth and early nineteenth centuries is a fascinating aspect of their later history which would repay a detailed study.

Castles and monasteries: common research themes

Shared research themes may be summarised in the context of the following techniques: documentary research, site recording and analysis, and materials analyses.

Documentary research: a thorough appraisal of the contents of existing research archives, identifying the gaps, and the accessioning and indexing of the material should be undertaken. Additional documentary research on both an area-wide basis and on specific sites may then be carried out. The foundation, construction, development, condition, repair, alteration, and reconstruction of castles and monasteries throughout the medieval and post-medieval periods can be charted with varying degrees of exactitude through a systematic study of the written, pictorial, and cartographic evidence. The Norman era offers the greatest uncertainties due to the paucity of records and the need for skilled professional interpretation of what survives. For the later medieval period the written sources are fuller and the evidence relatively good. Although a body of secondary literature exists which deals in varying degrees of depth with the history of castles and monasteries, this represents only a very small fraction of the evidence which is available. Any authoritative historical research must rest very largely on the primary manuscript sources.

Site recording and analysis: in general, earlier studies have been made in a somewhat haphazard fashion with little consistency in recording standards. Detailed analysis and interpretation of standing remains are now possible, partly as a consequence of the development of more accurate surveying and recording techniques. Most of the earlier plans of castles and monasteries derive from the work of a handful of surveyors, some with very fixed notions of their work. Properly drawn records, including surveying by photogrammetry, and 'stratigraphic' analysis of the fabric, linked to the evidence from documentary research and any diagnostic stylistic features, are now allowing fresh and sometimes completely different interpretations of what had been thought of as familiar and completely understood sites. In addition, the use of three-dimensional computer modelling is aiding reconstruction ideas and testing interpretations, as well as providing an impressive and informative medium for future presentation and education use.

Materials analyses: analysis of certain building materials can often provide essential corroborative information. Comprehensive dendrochronological sampling should provide sufficient evidence for the production of a detailed chronology of construction and refurbishment relating to the timber elements of castles and monasteries. In addition, it would provide more detailed information on the source of the timbers and perhaps identify distinct groups of timber within particular periods which would allow comparisons to be made with the documentary records. The evidence for woodland cover, management, and exploitation obtainable from the tree-ring sequences, may also allow for a greater understanding of the contemporary landscape when integrated with other archaeological and architectural information. Work could be planned to refine the descriptions of building stones through the preparation and microscopic examination of thin slices of stone samples. Comparative study of thin sections of samples from possible quarry sites may add weight to suggestions of provenance for building stones. As well as dendrochronological and petrological studies, analysis of other materials such as brick, mortar, glass, metal, plaster, daub, paint, and lichen, may provide technological or supplementary dating evidence.

Conclusion

In addition to the academic research objectives defined above, the continuing deterioration of our historic building stock through neglect, erosion, and pollution, emphasises the need for an accelerated programme of recording of standing fabric. For those sites in the management and care of public bodies, which have not been comprehensively recorded in recent years, the first stage should be the capture of accurate survey data. The resulting drawn and photographic records would then be available to aid detailed analysis and interpretation, as well as providing the basis for conservation and repair proposals. Initiatives from bodies such as English Heritage to encourage recording and analysis would provide an important first step towards the establishment of collaborative, long-term conservation and management schemes for those sites where the ownership of the remains is in the hands of local authorities or private individuals.

Despite several generations of study, our knowledge of the castles and monasteries of Lancashire has large gaps in it, and recent developments have made considerable changes to previously held views. The above is an attempt to help define options for further research in this field. The choice is inevitably based on personal experience. There are bound to be many alternative agenda and priorities. The shared aim, however, must be an achievable reality, using the rich resources which currently exist before embarking on new research initiatives in the wider study of the county's medieval and post-medieval history and archaeology.

References

Bu'Lock, J D, 1970 Churches, crosses, and mottes in the Lune Valley, *Archaeol Journ*, **127**, 291-92

Greene, J P, 1992 *Medieval monasteries*, Leicester

Greene, J P, forthcoming Monastic archaeology — strategies for future research and site investigation, in *The archaeology of monasteries* (ed G Keevill), Oxford

Higham, M C, 1991 The mottes of North Lancashire, Lonsdale, and South Cumbria, *Trans Cumberland Westmorland Antiq Archaeol Soc*, **91**, 79-90

King, D J C, 1983 *Castellarium Anglicanum — an index and bibliography of the castles in England, Wales, and the Islands*, v**1**, **2** New York

Knowles, D, and Hadcock, R N, 1971 *Medieval religious houses — England and Wales*, 2nd edn, London

Lott, B, 1995 Medieval buildings in Westmorland, unpubl PhD thesis, Univ Nottingham

Ordnance Survey, 1978 *Monastic Britain*, 3rd edn, London

10

INDUSTRIAL ARCHAEOLOGY

by Mark Fletcher

Despite major advances in recent years the archaeology of our industrial past, particularly that of the more recent past, has been sorely neglected by academic and professional archaeologists. Many academic institutions would prefer to pursue the more traditional archaeological periods, often concentrating their fieldwork on foreign territories. It is perhaps not difficult to understand such choices — fieldwork within St Helens, for instance, may not seem so pleasurable as a visit to a Roman city on the shores of the Mediterranean. What is more, academic archaeologists brought up on a diet of the distant past, may feel disadvantaged in dealing with technological topics which might seem to be more appropriately the province of engineers. This is, however, to misunderstand the nature of industrial archaeology. It is not simply about technology, but should seek to examine and study an industrial society through its material culture.

Until recently much of what was known about our industrial past was the result of the work of dedicated 'hobby' industrial archaeologists, but despite their efforts the industrial legacy of the pre-1974 county of Lancashire comprises a vast and poorly comprehended body of data. Yet its potential value as a mine of untapped scholarship is readily accessible to the willing researcher. The importance of this resource is confirmed by English Heritage, who recently stated that:

> 'If there is one archaeological topic in which England can claim to have international pre-eminence, it is in the industrial archaeology of the post-medieval period. The world heartland of the industrial revolution lies in midland and northern England, and England was one of the origins of the first large-scale mining, iron, and textile industries.' (English Heritage 1991).

There could be little dissent to the status of historical Lancashire as one of the cradles of modern industry, all authorities being in agreement that Manchester itself was the world's first industrial city, giving birth to the factory system of production. Yet despite this obvious importance, precious little research has been undertaken within this field. Only in recent years, following Ashmore's seminal works on the industrial North West (Ashmore 1982), and culminating with the recent RCHME-sponsored mill surveys (Williams with Farnie 1992), has the industrial heritage been taken seriously.

Many of our county Sites and Monuments Records (SMRs), in themselves the basis of our known archaeological resource, are sadly lacking in the content which reflects the richness of recent archaeological remains. Despite the importance of its industrial heritage, in the Lancashire County SMR out of a total of c11,000 entries, only about 20% relate to sites of industrial origin. This clearly reflects a shortfall in the perception of the traditional archaeological establishment to recognise the importance of such remains. Today, many archaeologists working in the North West prefer to doggedly persist in chasing the will o'the wisp of pre-industrial archaeology, without acknowledgment of the importance of the industrial heritage and oblivious to the massive ongoing attrition which is destroying the evidence for the origins of our industrial landscape.

Industrial development and decline

Although Lancashire was host to a plethora of interdependent industries commencing during the late eighteenth century, the cotton trade rose above all else to dominate both the bleak Pennine landscape and the world's trade markets. Partially mechanised textile production had occurred on a small scale in the North West during the medieval period, when water power was utilised to drive fulling hammers. During the 1770s, however, the development of the Arkwright spinning mills, initially on the Derbyshire Derwent and its tributaries (Menuge 1993), enormously accelerated the application of mechanisation within the textile industry. Several factors, including water power potential and the proximity of the fledgling port of Liverpool, caused this infant industry to gravitate to the Pennine slopes of Lancashire.

For its first few decades, this industry depended wholly upon water power, with many concerns being located in remote Pennine valleys. There was little apparent thought for how or where a workforce was to be housed. The fortuitous presence of the Lancashire Coalfield was a major factor in the geographical polarisation of what could have otherwise remained a short-lived rural phenomenon. In 1761 the completion of the Bridgewater Canal, between the Worsley mines and Castlefield in Manchester, resulted in a massive fall in the cost of coal haulage, thereby providing the economic incentive for an initially slow but inexorable development of steam power within the Manchester suburbs. By 1769 James Watt had patented the separate condenser (Dickinson and Jenkins 1981), a breakthrough which facilitated the only serious alternative to water power. The combination of these factors radically promoted the ascendancy of Manchester as the commercial centre of the Lancashire

By the mid-nineteenth century, steam power had liberated industry from its dependence upon the vagaries of water power, as demonstrated by this example of a large silk spinning mill at Galgate, near Lancaster, built in c 1852

textile trade, with almost 300 cotton towns and villages within a radius of 12 miles from the Royal Exchange.

Obviously, the knock-on effects of such rapid industrial growth were far-reaching. Following the 'canal mania' of the 1790s, transportation was revolutionised, encouraging the local development of industries essential to further growth of the textile trade, such as coal mining and heavy engineering. After 1830, further growth was aided by the expanding railway network. By the mid-nineteenth century, although the earlier waterside textile communities were still thriving, new steam-powered mill sites were locating on canals, railways, and roads, in tandem with new urban workforces living practically at the factory gates. This process was the catalyst for the origin of the archetypal industrial landscape of Lancashire.

Manchester itself achieved the distinction of becoming 'the first colossus born of a force that was changing the face of the world' (Roberts 1976). The emerging city underwent such vigorously rapid changes between 1800 and 1850 that contemporary chroniclers could only look on with awe. Even the immense number of steam powered factories which developed in the suburbs, were dwarfed by the growth of 'Cottonopolis', as an economic market of unchallenged supremacy.

The textile factories themselves evolved from almost domestic-scale workshops housing several hundred spindles in the late 1700s, to enormous complexes of multi-storeyed and highly embellished buildings by 1900, each housing perhaps over 100,000 spindles. The area also became characterised by regional specialisation within the industry, with Manchester and its satellite towns, such as Bolton and Oldham, being dominated by spinning, while North East Lancashire concentrated upon weaving, in places such as Blackburn and Burnley.

The zenith of industrial Lancashire was achieved in 1926, when Liverpool docks unloaded over three million raw-cotton bales, and almost 600,000 people were employed in scores of factories. The world depression of 1929–32, coupled with the development of textile industries overseas — ironically largely aided by Lancashire machine-making firms — ensured that by the 1960s the UK had become a net importer of cotton goods (Williams with Farnie 1992; Clarke 1985).

The relentless requirement for technological improvement within the cotton industry, had ensured that Lancashire occupied the cutting edge of engineering developments during the late eighteenth and early nineteenth centuries. Richard Arkwright had patented a whole series of cotton-spinning machines, the royalties from which made him a personal fortune; on the other hand Samuel Crompton's spinning mule, vastly superior to the Arkwright water-frame, left its inventor impoverished. Incentives for innovation had all manner of motivation — the engineer Richard Roberts was employed by a group of Manchester mill owners to develop a self-acting spinning mule, in order to curtail the bargaining power of their spinning mule operators. He succeeded brilliantly between 1825 and 1830, and the mill owners regained their ascendancy.

The patents of Boulton and Watt did not expire until 1800, and although Manchester engineers flouted the law, or otherwise circumvented the patents, it is probable that the further development of the steam-engine was curtailed until this stranglehold was lifted. The great millwright Wren, and his one-time apprentice Fairbairn, worked from Manchester, the latter taking the development of the waterwheel to its ultimate form, as well as improving upon boilers and steam engines. The partnership of Fairbairn with Eaton Hodgkinson, during the 1820s, resulted in significant steps in the utilisation of cast-iron for structural purposes. These included the so-called 'fireproof mill' buildings, and increasingly after c1830, the development of railway bridges (Fitzgerald 1987).

Naturally, with the ever-increasing demand for textile machinery, it is not surprising that Lancashire became a nationally important centre for the development and manufacture of machine tools. Initially, such work was undertaken by joiners and clock-makers, but during the early nineteenth century specialist firms of engineers were established to meet the requirements of the cotton trade. These were set up by the previously-mentioned Richard Roberts, and others like James Nasmyth, and Joseph Whitworth, the latter achieving worldwide distinction for his standardisation of screw threads (George 1977).

The other major Lancashire industry, linked closely to textiles as an energy provider, was coal mining. Small-scale exploitation of coal from the Lancashire Coalfield was known to have occurred from the medieval period onwards, but the demand for fuel to run mill boilers after c1800 resulted in mining on an unprecedented scale. In the 1750s the millwright Brindley created a water-driven pumping system at Wet Earth Colliery, Salford; using a brilliantly engineered headrace from the Irwell, with an inverted syphon cut through solid bedrock to force the water supply hydraulically beneath the river gorge. This allowed coal winning from a much greater depth than was previously possible by sough drainage.

The real challenge to Lancashire's miners lay in being able to mine to hundreds and even thousands of feet in depth, and the joint problems of drainage, winding, and ventilation at these limits were only overcome by the application of steam power during the early nineteenth century. The use of steam power in coal mining went hand-in-hand with its application in textiles manufacture. Because of the bulk of the raw product, the influence of transport improvements upon coal mining was enormous, and these fossil reserves could only be exploited on a large-scale for export out of the coalfield after the growth of the canal and railway networks. The coal mining industry spawned its own indigenous landscape across most of upland Lancashire, one of headstocks and spoil heaps, and ultimately one of devastation and dereliction, as the mining industry vanished when the demand for coal disappeared.

Other, smaller industries, usually linked to textiles or coal, thrived across Lancashire. These included metal trades, quarrying, chemicals, soap, glass, papermaking, and others too numerous to mention.

The eventual decline of Lancashire's industrial infrastructure was swift and inexorable. Largely presaged by the Great Depression of 1929–32, this process became irreversible between c1960 and 1990, highlighted by such memorable events as the Beeching Act of 1963 which dismantled much of the railway system. Closures of textile mills and engineering works became everyday events, and as recently as 1988 the last self-acting mule ceased to run in Ramsbottom. The demolition of the headstocks of Parkside Colliery, St Helens, in 1995, represented the final death knell of the Lancashire coal mining industry.

Industrial communities

Initially, at the onset of industrialisation, the effects on the population were limited. During the late eighteenth and early nineteenth centuries, members of rural-based families would find employment near to their homes in water-powered textile mills, or small-scale coal mines. The widespread application of steam power after *c*1830, however, demanded that an ever-expanding and disciplined pool of labour was required to be close to the workplace, and in many rural locations purpose-built villages were established, replete with employer-owned facilities such as shops, schools, churches, libraries, and institutes. Increasingly, however, industrial communities were located within the suburbs of the older towns, encroaching upon one another, to form urban landscapes of terraced housing dominated by the vast bulk of the mills which they served.

During the early nineteenth century, the acute problem of a locally available workforce was solved by immigration of farm workers from East Anglia and Ireland in particular, or by the apprenticing of pauper children from workhouses in Birmingham and London. Many of these new urbanites were to suffer appalling living conditions, with their work comprising hard, long hours of toil in noisy, dirty, and often dangerous conditions in mills and mines.

Under such conditions workers unrest fermented — a few made vast fortunes, while the rest lived in squalor and poverty, as witnessed by Engels in Manchester in 1842:

> 'The race that lives in these ruinous cottages, behind broken windows, mended with oilskin, sprung doors, and rotten door-posts, or in dark, wet cellars, in measureless filth and stench, in this atmosphere penned in as if with a purpose, this race must really have reached the lowest stages of humanity.' (quoted in Trinder 1982).

Disaffection with their condition inevitably led the masses into agitation, if not outright revolt, during the years of 1811–50. The Luddite crisis of 1811–13 was followed by the Peterloo massacre of 1819, while Owenite propaganda, demands for Parliamentary reform, the Ten Hours Movement, and Chartism, characterised the following decades (Thompson 1963).

During the formative years of the industrial revolution, many self-contained rural communities were to develop in close proximity to factories dependent upon water supply. Belmont village is a good example, situated on a bleak Pennine hillside overlooking the Dye Works in the valley below

Until the formation of joint stock companies after *c*1860 the means of industrial production were invariably concentrated within individual families, many of which became immensely wealthy. These newly-empowered industrial magnates were to challenge the established landed gentry for positions of authority. The Peel family, of yeoman stock, generated a vast fortune before 1800 from a series of spinning and bleaching mills on the River Irwell to the north of Manchester. Their influence extended to the highest echelons of government, with the grandson of the first entrepreneur achieving the post of Prime Minister. Some of these family dynasties recognised a need for philanthropy, the Ashworth family constructing a self-contained village by their mill at Egerton, which became a showpiece of paternalistic benevolence to visitors. Such colonies were invariably rural based, however, and elsewhere the evidence would suggest that attitudes towards the workforce varied from indifference to outright exploitation.

The drive towards industrialisation has left an imprint upon the physical landscape of Lancashire which is now immeasurable in terms of scale and extent. Contemporary literature can only hint at whatever social and economic upheavals prevailed during this revolutionary period. The surviving evidence for this process is, however, physically vulnerable and is ultimately susceptible to the losses which afflict all of our historic fabric.

Threats to the surviving evidence

Although the physical evidence is still manifested across our landscape in great quantities, the threats to the survival of Lancashire's industrial fabric are both insidious and formidable. Industrial buildings commonly disappear under the constant pressure for redevelopment, or suffer wholesale refurbishment, where evidence for previous use is obliterated without record. This is particularly true of insensitive mill conversions, yet the implementation of restrictive planning conditions only discourages their reuse and hastens their decline and eventual loss. To survive these structures must be used, for without use they will cease to have value and without value no amount of conservation inspired management will sustain them. Within Greater Manchester Metropolitan county, an average of two large mills per month were demolished during the 1980s, many of these having not been recorded at all. Post-Second World War slum clearance has removed the vast swathes of early dwellings which housed the long-disappeared proletariat now immortalised by the works of Engels, Gaskell, Roberts, and Lowry.

Industrial landscapes are equally at threat. Natural decay of fabric has resulted in dozens of picturesque, but unrecorded ruins in the remote Pennine valleys. Large-scale clearance of derelict land equally destroys or obscures archaeological remains, including those below ground. The redevelopment of central St Helens removed, along with vast quantities of industrial contamination, many metres of archaeological stratigraphy relating to the town's industrial past, most of which was removed without record. The value of river valleys for newer industrial developments results in massive destruction of early water-based industrial sites. In a similar vein, well-meaning but poorly-managed excavation and conservation projects engender a similar end result, with evidence being commonly lost, or simply not being recognised.

Fieldwork is obviously required to record the physical remains still present, but other methods are required to augment and amplify the physical record. Industrial processes are poorly documented, but still in our midst are some of the mill hands, miners, and other workers, many now retired, who provide the last dwindling human links to describe just how these jobs were actually done. Similarly, the surviving archived documentary material which chronicles the workings of industrial Lancashire could probably be measured as a tiny fraction of those records originally generated.

The Mersey railway in Stockport represents a civil engineering achievement of immense scale. The viaduct width has been increased by almost as much again, the difference in brickwork being visible beneath the arches, and the demolition of Wear Mill was avoided by spanning over the top of it

The monuments to industrial greatness

Across the North West, the physical evidence for the industrial period is clearly apparent, not only in the acres of devastation resulting from mining and quarrying, but also in the spectacular surviving monuments which characterise this landscape, a contrast with, and the equal of, the great medieval churches and castles which dominate the heritage of other regions. The gaunt steam-powered mills of the Ancoats complex have survived as Listed Buildings within a suburb of Manchester, preserving a rare glimpse of the embryonic factory system. On the edge of Castlefield, the 1830 Railway Warehouse, now integrated as part of the Greater Manchester Museum of Science and Industry, is recognised as of international importance as an element of the first passenger railway in the world, connecting Manchester with Liverpool.

The Manchester Ship Canal, completed in 1894, broke the monopoly of the Liverpool Docks over the cotton trade. It remains an engineering feat of staggering proportions, the bulk of the excavation works having been undertaken by hand. Equally impressive is the Mersey railway viaduct, just to the west of Stockport town centre, standing 34 metres above the river, and spanning the valley on 26 arches, beneath one of which stands a large cotton mill.

Similarly, the small town of Darwen is dominated, somewhat incongruously, by the colossal campanile stack of India Mill, which rises to over 90 metres, now functioning only as a mausoleum to the vanished cotton trade. Less than a mile to the south is the massive earthwork which once impounded Jacks Key Reservoir, formerly known as 'Weavers' Rest', reflecting the number of local textile workers who chose to end their lives there.

At Harle Syke Mill, Queen Street, in Burnley, an *in situ* horizontal steam engine has survived to drive the last working Lancashire weaving shed, and the casual visitor is briefly subjected to the same barrage of deafening noise which afflicted the loom operatives long before the Health and Safety at Work Act was drafted.

A monument of a less obvious nature is the Cheesden Valley, a deep glacial gorge which straddles the modern boundary between Lancashire and Greater Manchester. Here, because of remoteness from modern redevelopment, an early nineteenth century industrial landscape, albeit ruined, has survived intact, with remains of textile mills, dwellings, coal mines, trackways, and other features (Sandiford and Ashworth 1981). Moves to ensure wholesale statutory preservation may have foundered, but the landscape remains fossilised as a unique source of information on early industrialisation.

It is important to recognise that we, in the closing years of the twentieth century, are in a unique and privileged position, in that we are witness to the death throes of the industrial society upon which the modern world is based. If we are to realise any opportunity to both record and preserve aspects of that society, then it is important to act now. No amount of learned discussion or debate can act as a substitute for the necessity to take positive steps while the evidence is still manifest.

The research agenda

Lancashire's industrial archaeology is clearly definable, both in terms of visible remains and chronological context. Its genesis was that of an indigenous, home-grown culture, with little foreign influence, and its ramifications spread to assume global significance. Yet although much of the physical infrastructure appeared to have been constructed to function for centuries, the whole process of industrialisation was over

Costing £14,000 and completed in 1867, the chimney of India Mill, Darwen, 'is perhaps the most remarkable architectural achievement of the whole [cotton] industry' (Aspin 1995)

within a few generations. As a subject for future archaeological and historical study, it could have few serious parallels within the North West, or within Britain.

Much of the existing corpus of research material is necessarily limited both in terms of geography and subject matter. What is clearly lacking at the moment is even a superficial assessment of the most important categories of surviving evidence. This cannot be gleaned from the woefully inadequate records contained within county SMRs, but requires much new research both in the field and in archive collections.

The Association for Industrial Archaeology recently published a policy document for the objectives of industrial archaeology in the 1990s (Palmer 1991), this summarises both the scope of the subject, and makes recommendations for further works to pursue those objectives. In the light of this document suggested research topics across the pre-1974 Lancashire county could address the following questions:

- do distributions of water-powered textile mill sites reflect pre-industrial utilisation of the same sites by medieval or post-medieval corn or fulling mills?

- how were successive patterns of industrial development affected by improvements in transportation networks and the progressive exploitation of the Lancashire Coalfield?

- how quickly did technological innovation disseminate itself across industries, and by what means, and is this innovation reflected within surviving remains? For example how was the concept of the fireproof mill diffused through Lancashire?

- why and how did regional specialisation occur within the textile industry? For example what lay behind the mid-nineteenth century development of the cotton-weaving belt between Burnley and Colne?

- what was the nature of the workforce in the early development of the industrial settlements, did they have rural roots and are these evidenced in their material culture and their use of domestic space?

- how were early industrial settlements organised?

- how was housing provided for the workers, and how did their dwellings develop; the old county of Lancashire has yet to benefit from the comprehensive surveys to which West Yorkshire has recently been subjected (Caffyn 1986; Sheeran 1993).

Many years of research could be expended in attempting to answer some of these questions, it would be most cost-effective to initiate any programme by means of a rapid desk-based assessment to enhance the SMRs and to determine which categories of both physical remains and documentary records survive in sufficient quantities to merit further research. Of particular interest would be the origins and development of industries in the towns. The surviving urban fabric is manifested as a palimpsest of repeated industrial redevelopment, each episode partially erasing the traces of earlier phases. Lancashire's urbanism is primarily a result of the industrial revolution and it is in towns that modern redevelopment is removing the evidence most rapidly. There is then an urgent need to catalogue what exists and to assess its importance; to some extent this is being done by English Heritage in their Monuments Protection Programme, but this is a national initiative and necessarily superficial. The RCHME have taken a clear lead in the recording of industrial remains, in particular that of surviving textile mills across the north of England. They have recently highlighted priority areas for future work on a national basis (Falconer 1993), including the lack of an adequate study of the surviving mills of modern Lancashire and Cumbria.

The necessary resources to finance the outlined research framework must be partly found through developer-funded archaeology, but for this to meet the needs of Lancashire's industrial archaeology will require co-ordination with programmes financed by both central and local government. Nevertheless, the existence of research aims could and should be utilised within the planning process to trigger funding as a consequence of public utility or private development.

References

Ashmore, O, 1982 *The industrial archaeology of North West England,* Manchester

Caffyn, L, 1986 *Workers' housing in West Yorkshire, 1750–1920,* London

Clarke, A, 1985 *The effects of the Factory System,* London

Dickinson, H W, and Jenkins, R, 1981 *James Watt and the steam engine,* Ashbourne

English Heritage, 1991 *Exploring our past. Strategies for the archaeology of England,* London

Falconer, K A, 1993 Textile mills and the RCHME, *Ind Archaeol Rev,* **16,** 5–50

Fitzgerald, R S, 1987 The development of the Cast Iron Frame, in Textile mills to 1850, *Ind Archaeol Rev,* **10,** 127–145

George, A D, 1977 *An introduction to the Industrial Archaeology of Manchester and South Lancashire,* Manchester

Menuge, A, 1993 The cotton mills of the Derbyshire Derwent and its tributaries, *Ind Archaeol Rev,* **16,** 38–61

Palmer, M, 1991 *Industrial archaeology — working for the future,* Assoc Ind Archaeol

Roberts, R, 1976 *A ragged schooling,* Manchester

Sandiford, A V, and Ashworth, T E, 1981 *The forgotten valley,* Bury

Sheeran, G, 1993 *Brass castles — West Yorkshire new rich and their houses 1800–1914,* Keele

Thompson, E P, 1963 *The making of the English working class,* London

Trinder, B, 1982 *The making of the industrial landscape,* London

Williams, M, with Farnie, D A, 1992 *Cotton mills in Greater Manchester,* Preston

11

THE FUTURE FOR LANCASHIRE'S ARCHAEOLOGY

by Graeme Bell

The Past

Archaeologists, of all people, do not need to be reminded that before looking forward, one should reflect on the past! The long history of settlement over most of Lancashire has resulted in a very ancient landscape with associated features. Evidence of prehistoric hunter gatherers and early pastoralists have been uncovered across the county, and in the Bronze Age the first signs of organised settlement appear. During the Roman occupation Lancashire formed part of a militarized zone supporting the military presence on the northern frontier. The medieval period saw the establishment of much of our present settlement pattern, road system, and other landscape features. Medieval Lancashire played a pivotal role in the history and development of England; the legacy from this period is still present in the county in the form of castles and manor houses. Lancashire also enjoys the privilege of being amongst the first industrial societies in the world, and the structures relating to this great period may be observed in most of our towns and some villages.

The Present

The current arrangements for investigating, managing, and curating Lancashire's archaeological resource are a cat's cradle of responsibilities. There is no military chain of command; statutory duties are discharged at variable levels of effectiveness; central government agencies and academic bodies have assumed roles in key areas. If all the organisations and agencies play to their strengths and in close harmony, then it is a formidable team (Diagram 1). However, it is a matter of debate in which league Lancashire archaeology is playing at the present time. A 'Health Check' (Diagram 2) of the team suggests that there are many weaknesses and threats. Equally, there are strengths and opportunities, if there is a will to change things for the better.

The Future

The publication of PPG16 Archaeology and Planning (DoE 1990) and PPG 15 Historic Buildings and Landscapes (DoE and DNH 1994) gives renewed emphasis to the role of town and country planning in this area (Diagram 3). For the last few years discussions have been underway between English Heritage and the county and district councils to see how this may be formalised. The position and long-term secure funding for the Sites and Monuments Record (SMR) is central to this debate. Unfortunately, this comes at a time when resources for all public services are under increasing constraint and imagination and lateral thinking will be needed to see how the circle can be squared. The future will almost certainly rely on a partnership of public and private, professional and amateur, statutory and non-statutory arrangements.

Such an arrangement demands strong, clear leadership and direction, to ensure that the challenge to protect and conserve Lancashire's archaeological heritage is met. The day school at which this paper was delivered, in May 1995, was a valuable first step in establishing the network of contacts and supports needed to identify a champion who will lead the alliance.

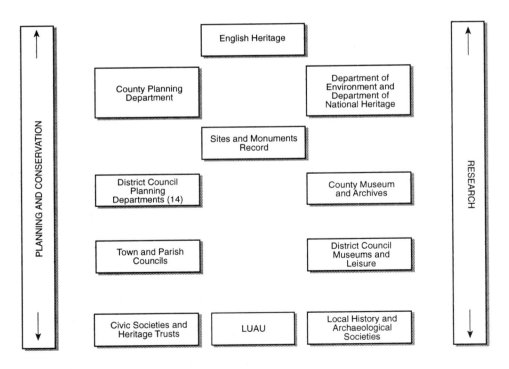

Diagram 1. Lancashire Archaeologists: The Team of all the Talents

Strengths
>   Dedicatedpeople
>   Lancaster University — centre of excellence
>   Track record of achievement
>   Strong local attachment to the Palatine
>   Retention of present local authority structure

Weaknesses
>   Under resourced
>   Poor chain of command
>   Multi-agency responsiblity
>   Lack of a champion — John O'Gaunt II needed!

Opportunities
>   Partnerships to succeed
>   PPG16 and PPG15 — a breakthrough for planning?
>   Sustainable Development
>   European intervention and funding
>   Millenium/Heritage nostalgia
>   Lottery bids

Threats
>   Shortage of resources
>   Compulsory competitive tendering
>   Overshadowed by more 'popular' green issues
>   Self doubt

Diagram 2. Lancashire Archaeology: Health Check

Since May 1995 major steps have been taken to secure and improve the provision of archaeological services in Lancashire. The SMR which has been curated by Lancaster University since 1976 will, from April 1996, be operated through the Planning Department of Lancashire County Council. This will enable Lancashire County Council to integrate the archaeological information with its other environmental data sources and to provide advice on the archaeological implications of development as part of its routine planning procedures. The increased resources that will be available in the county authority, the improved access to district authority planning departments and the better co-operation with other environmental interests that will result from being in the county authority, will enable the SMR to provide an enhanced and improved service.

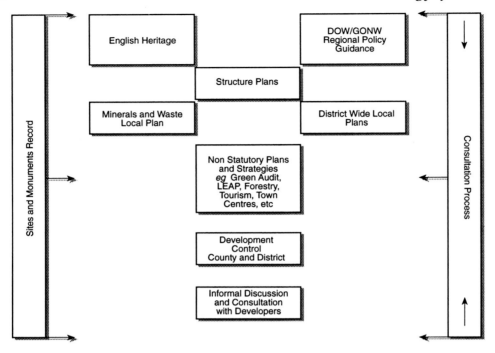

Diagram 3. Lancashire Archaeology: Town and Country Planning Framework Policy, Plans and Practice

The removal of the SMR from Lancaster University will also remove the impediment of the Archaeological Unit being perceived as both a curator and a contractor. Naturally developers are suspicious of employing archaeologists to undertake work specified by planning authorities whose advice is seemingly derived from the same archaeologists. This can no longer be seen as the case.

The resources devoted to Lancashire's archaeology are now greater and better integrated than ever before. Nevertheless, we should not be complacent, there are many challenges to be met. At a broad level these include:

•   conserving the heritage resource whilst encouraging the development, both for the future benefit of the county;

•   the possible implications of rising sea levels and coastal erosion as a result of global warming;

- the maintenance of quality archaeological services in a competitive, cost-conscious environment.

References

DoE, 1990 *Archaeology and planning; Planning Policy Guidance Note,* **16**, London

DoE and DNH 1994 *Planning and the historic environment; Planning Policy Guidance Note,* **15**, London

12

PRIORITIES AND CHALLENGES

by Peter Iles and Richard Newman

The conference on Lancashire Archaeology clearly revealed the need to put in place research objectives to inform an essentially response-led programme of archaeological work. By highlighting the important areas of current research needs, archaeological curators can be assisted in assessing the implications of development. Without a regional research agenda it can be all too easy to continually respond to development threats in a piecemeal fashion, biasing the responses towards what is already known at the expense of the unknown. In particular this leads to the neglect of areas where little or no archaeological material has been recovered or reported.

If resources for archaeological investigation were unlimited, perhaps such considerations would be less important, but resources are, and always will be, constrained. Thus there is a need to prioritise, focusing these limited resources on those areas that are likely to be most productive in new information and insights. Put crudely, it may be more important to record a post-medieval industrial site that was key to a community's development and of a type not well recorded elsewhere, rather than to undertake a limited excavation of a medieval or prehistoric site type that has been frequently examined.

It should be borne in mind, however, that most types of site will display regional variations, and though a site type may be well studied in one region, in another region work will be lacking. For this reason regional research agendas are probably of more use than national ones. A significant problem with English Heritage's *Exploring our past* (1991) was that too many archaeologists took it as a national research agenda rather than a document highlighting themes, the application and relevance of which varies from place to place.

In Lancashire there are clear gaps in our knowledge at the most basic level, and these need to be addressed before some of the more developed research issues put forward by English Heritage (1991), and even thirteen years ago by the Council for British

Archaeology (Thomas 1983), can be explored. We cannot ignore the old adage that 'absence of evidence is not evidence of absence'. Before even considering this, however, we need to know whether or not the limits of our present knowledge are a result of a genuine lack of evidence or a want of looking.

Lancashire has not been as actively investigated as many other areas, particularly before the the creation of the archaeology unit at Lancaster University. This is most graphically illustrated in English Heritage's review of government sponsored rescue excavations between 1938 to 1972. Post-1974 Lancashire has only one site listed, Ribchester, Greater Manchester also only has one and Merseyside a meagre two. From the viewpoint of central government funding of site investigations before 1973, these three counties were the least investigated in England (Butcher and Garwood 1994, 79-80). Compare their numbers with Northamptonshire 53, Wiltshire 52, or even to avoid suspicions of a southern bias, North Yorkshire with 43 sites (*ibid*, 80-82). Since the late 1970s the pace of archaeological research in Lancashire has increased, and as this volume demonstrates concerns and interests have come forward in time from a narrow focus on prehistoric and Roman issues only. What is more, projects such as the North West Wetlands Survey have helped to redress the imbalance in central government-financed archaeological research, with considerable resources being spent in the North West in recent years. Nevertheless, significant gaps still exist in our knowledge of Lancashire's archaeological heritage.

Lacunae

Our knowledge of prehistoric settlements and landscapes from the Mesolithic through to the end of the Bronze Age is still very patchy. There is a discrepancy between the type of evidence recovered from the lowlands, and that from the uplands. The distribution of the sites in the uplands is particularly problematic because of the masking effects of overlying blanket peats, or heather moorlands, in many areas. The upland site distributions also appear to better reflect the activities of past archaeologists, than they do the distribution of real sites. The concentration of sites on Worsthorne Moor, for example, is a result of that area having been investigated (Leach 1951), not a result of that area's attractiveness for prehistoric activity. The lowlands have also had more recent palaeoecological sampling in comparison to the uplands. Overall, however, there is a lack of clear linkages between palaeoecological evidence and excavated archaeological materials

The situation after about *c* 800 BC until at least the eighth century AD, is even more dire. With the exception of Roman military sites, we know next to nothing about the peoples inhabiting Lancashire from the Iron Age through to the inclusion of the area into the kingdom of Northumbria. This may itself say something about the likely continuity of the cultural environment. Beyond patterns of Anglian and Scandinavian

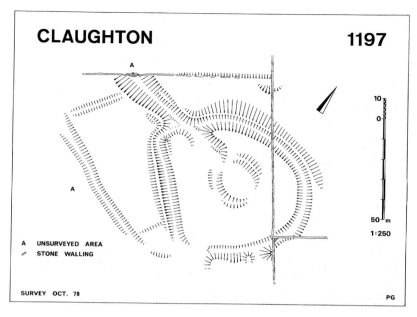

Plan of the probable Iron Age enclosure at Claughton, near Lancaster

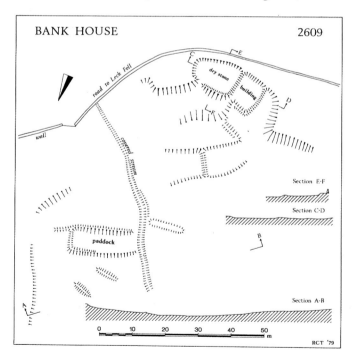

Plan of Bank House earthwork; similar to, and possibly part of, the extensive prehistoric settlements on Leck Fell, near Kirkby Lonsdale

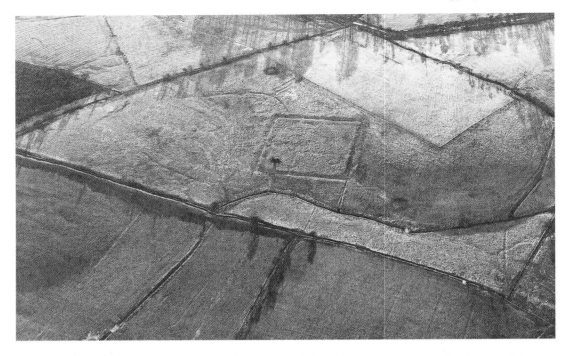

*Bomber Camp, near Barnoldswick, excavated in 1939, and considered to be possibly
Romano-British*

place-names, isolated examples of sculpture and architecture, and a few largely
unhelpful references in the documentary record, we know little more about the period
from the ninth to the eleventh centuries.

After the Norman Conquest, increasing documentation and the survival of some
masonry monuments tells us a little about the economy and society of the elite, but
for the mass of Lancashire's rural population we continue to lack a detailed knowledge
of their livelihoods and the landscapes they inhabited and influenced. We know little
about the physical nature and material culture of the rural settlements, and without
an established medieval pottery sequence, our chronologies are vague. Because of
this it is difficult to assess how medieval communities evolved and developed out of
the earlier societies, nor how they influenced and are incorporated into the fabric of
today's settlement pattern.

Threats

In certain areas of research, Lancashire has been in the forefront. Through the study
of its wetlands Lancashire has a considerable body of palaeoecological data relating

to prehistoric land-use in the lowlands. The archaeological study of its buildings, particularly those dating to the medieval period, is also more advanced than in many areas, allowing specific and in-depth research questions to be asked. Moreover, the county also contains abundant, if unassessed, evidence for some key areas of archaeological interest. In particular it still retains many physical remains of nineteenth-century industrialisation and urbanism. These resources however, are being eroded at a frighteningly rapid rate.

Lancashire, outside of the coastal plain — and particularly the Fylde — is fortunate in comparison to some counties in being dominated by pastoral farming. This means that the damage occasioned by annual deep ploughing is limited, though ancient pastures are, on occasion, ploughed for re-seeding, a potential Iron Age site at Chipping was damaged recently in just this way. Even so, overall, rural sites in the pasture-dominated areas of the county are better protected than sites in arable farming regions, but as a consequence, the opportunities for site discovery through surface artefact recovery are much more limited. Nevertheless, Lancashire's archaeological resource faces continual erosion from many sources, only some of which can be monitored and controlled through the planning process.

Of these threats the most prevalent is new construction, either for industrial or housing needs. In a county such as Lancashire, which has suffered greatly in the latter half of the twentieth century from the wholesale decay of traditional industries, new industry is to be encouraged. Unfortunately, whether new industries are located on green field sites or are situated in areas of derelict former industry, adverse impacts on the archaeological resource can and do occur. Green field sites are at risk, particularly if no known archaeological remains are associated with them. The current practice in many local authorities is not to require any form of archaeological investigations in such circumstances, this means that archaeological work is targeted towards known sites, ensuring a future distributional bias in the archaeological record for the county. Even where assessments of archaeological potential are required, the needs of the developer will often override the requirements of conservation. An example of this is the recent destruction — although thankfully with record — of a significant stretch of Roman road east of Preston by a large, new paper processing unit. Redevelopment of existing facilities, which from an economic perspective is to be encouraged, will inevitably remove archaeological remains, for example the redundant Leyland Motors works at Farrington is to be cleared and rejuvenated as a business park. Any redevelopment in the centres of the textile towns, Blackburn, Burnley, or Accrington for instance; may well have an archaeological dimension relating to industrial remains or even their associated urban dwellings.

The refurbishment of buildings for domestic or other use is another major threat to the survival of standing archaeological remains in Lancashire. Barns and former textile mills are both regularly converted, churches and chapels modified and re-used. If the resulting alterations are unsympathetic, the damage wrought can be enormous but it must be remembered that if these buildings are not re-used they may well decay and fall down. The requirements of a modern society for housing, leisure, transport, and the provision of utilities, result in numerous other threats to the archaeological resource, from golf courses and community forests, to pipelines and rural infill developments. The needs of society must be met, it is neither practical nor desirable to conserve everything, but where damage or destruction of the archaeological resource is inevitable, recording and analysis should take place. Provision is made for this in Planning Policy Guidance Notes 15 and 16 (DoE 1991; DoE and DNH 1994), issued by the Department of the Environment and the Department of National Heritage. Correctly implemented these policies should ensure that full consideration is given to the archaeological implications of development, and, where recording is necessary and appropriate, that such work is funded within the development process. Unless archaeologists are simply to respond to a threat-led agenda, however, they need to regard these requirements for archaeological intervention as opportunities to answer the questions posed by the gaps in our knowledge.

Weaver's house, Bacup (courtesy of P D Iles)

Research Priorities

One of the greatest challenges facing archaeologists in Lancashire is the lack of available data over large swathes of the county. Addressing this would both aid the development of research agendas and enable better responses to threats to the archaeological resource. Rapid identification surveys are urgently needed for many areas. Very few large sections of landscape have been subjected to these, the largest being the North West Wetlands Survey which has concentrated on the lowland peat mosses. The Arnside/Silverdale Area of Outstanding Natural Beauty has been surveyed (LUAU 1993), as have parts of the Lune Valley — although the results have never been formally assessed. In the uplands, Anglezarke and Rivington Moors have been surveyed (Howard-Davis and Quartermaine forthcoming), and most recently North West Water's Bowland estate. The only other major completed landscape survey in the county is that of the Cowpe Valley in Rossendale, which was only examined for its industrial archaeology (LUAU 1996). The county still lacks an adequately assessed aerial photographic coverage and many areas covered in the uplands are difficult to interpret, because of heather and deep peat ground cover. Infra-red aerial photography as well as producing excellent results for cropmark complexes, can also be used to distinguish archaeological remains beneath heather, and this maybe an approach that can be used in the future.

Some previous archaeological work, particularly from before the 1980s, continues to languish in unassessed, unpublished, archives. Other useful data, though available in the SMR is not available in published form — the converse is also true — and analysis and interpretation of some of the information gathered in the many assessments and evaluations undertaken in the past decade, would add greatly to our knowledge of particular areas. As previously highlighted by Jason Wood (*see Chapter 9 this volume*), the information available in old archives and more recent unpublished assessments of medieval monasteries, could, if taken together, lead to a significant analysis of these sites.

Very little is known about the pre-industrial development of Lancashire's towns. Equally a full appreciation of the remains relating to the industrial revolution in these towns is still required. Yet it is within Lancashire's urban areas that the majority of development activity is currently concentrated. There is, therefore, an urgent requirement to quantify the scale and nature of the archaeological resource within these towns. In Lancaster English Heritage's proposed funding of an urban database will be greatly beneficial in this respect, but the other historic towns should not be forgotten. In particular documentary and map-based assessments should be undertaken for all of the county's urban areas.

Whilst Lancashire's industrial remains are not confined solely to urban areas, map-based assessments of all the major areas of industrial activity will be greatly beneficial, though the work of individuals such as Mike Rothwell and the various local societies is already very useful in this respect. Unfortunately, not all the local researchers in this field forward their results directly to the SMR, and thus the wider archaeological public are denied access to their findings, also the assessment of development threats is hampered. Of particular importance in Lancashire are the remains of the textile industry, and given the rate of redevelopment and in some cases destruction of the textile mills and their attendant industrial complexes, a survey of these sites to set priorities for detailed recording is long overdue.

The development of Lancashire's rural settlements and their farming infrastructures is little understood before the post-medieval period. Only excavation in combination with palaeoenvironmental sampling will improve the situation with regard to prehistoric settlements. In particular there is a need to investigate a range of lowland sites at present only recognised as surface artefact scatters. From the Iron Age onwards, surviving earthworks often provide the evidence for former settlements. In the uplands many earthwork sites have still not been surveyed in detail, and even when surveyed such sites can only be interpreted by their morphological affinities with similar sites elsewhere. Such an approach precludes the close dating of these sites nor does it reveal much about the economy and society of the inhabitants. Again excavation, preferably in tandem with palaeoecological sampling, is required to enlighten this situation. The study of medieval settlements and agriculture can also be advance through the morphological assessment of existing villages and of their surrounding landscapes.

The study of rural settlement clearly highlights the need for an holistic approach unfettered by conventional period divisions. In a region such as Lancashire, where settlement and agricultural activities have been severely constrained by environmental factors, it is quite likely that similar approaches and strategies were adopted over many millennia. In such circumstances both period and site-specific research methodologies are inadequate, an issue emphasised by the CBA nationally in 1983 (Thomas 1983) but one that still needs to be addressed in the North West.

Conclusion

As has been made clear by Graeme Bell (*see Chapter 11 this volume*) the provision of a strategic overview for managing Lancashire's archaeological resource has been lacking. Throughout the late 1980s and early 1990s, the SMR was too busy dealing with the day-to-day business of providing development control advice to be able to take time out to identify archaeological priorities and *lacunae*. Apart from work sponsored by English Heritage and some personal research projects, most archaeological work in Lancashire was reactive, responding to threats posed by development in an essentially *ad hoc* manner. The need for work was not generally assessed against the percieved requirements for archaeological research in the county.

The recent changes in the organisation of the archaeological curation service in the county should enable a more considered and integrated approach to be given to the management of Lancashire's archaeological resource. Central to this should be the formulation and application of research priorities. Hopefully, this present volume will represent a small step in this process.

References

Butcher, S, and Garwood, P, 1994 *Rescue excavation 1938 to 1972*, London

DoE, 1990 *Archaeology and planning; Planning Policy Guidance Note*, **16**, London

DoE and DNH, 1994 *Planning and the Historic Environment; Planning Policy Guidance Note*, **15**, London

English Heritage, 1991 *Exploring our past*, London

Howard-Davis, C, and Quartermaine, J, forthcoming Survey on Anglezarke Moor and the excavation of an early Mesolithic site at Rushy Brow, *Proc Prehist Soc*

Leach, G B, 1951 Flint implements from the Worsthorne Moors, Lancashire, *Trans Hist Soc Lancashire Cheshire*, **103**, 1-32

LUAU, 1993 *Arnside/Silverdale AONB: Cumbria and Lancashire rapid identification survey*, unpubl client report

LUAU, 1996 *The Industrial Archaeology of Rossendale*, unpubl client report

Thomas, C (ed), 1983 *Research objectives in British archaeology*, London

Index